IF FISH COULD
SCREAM

AN ANGLER'S SEARCH FOR THE FUTURE OF FLY FISHING

PAUL SCHULLERY

STACKPOLE
BOOKS

Published by
STACKPOLE BOOKS
5067 Ritter Road
Mechanicsburg, PA 17055
www.stackpolebooks.com

Printed in the United States

First edition

Photographs by the author
Angler protraits by Marsha Karle
With additional illustrations from angling literature

10 9 8 7 6 5 4 3 2 1

Library of Congress Cataloging-in-Publication Data

Schullery, Paul.
  If fish could scream : American fly fishing and how it got that way /
Paul Schullery. — 1st ed.
      p. cm.
  Includes bibliographical references and index.
  ISBN-13: 978-0-8117-0435-9 (hardcover)
  ISBN-10: 0-8117-0435-1 (hardcover)
  1. Fly fishing—United States. I. Title.

SH463.S33 2007
799.12'40973—dc22
                                            2007042083

for Ken Cameron

TABLE OF CONTENTS

For many anglers, fly fishing empowers an intensely personal experience of rivers: "Pick up your fly rod, stand facing the river, and the world opens out from there." Angler Bob DeMott faces the river in the Gallatin Valley, Montana. AUTHOR PHOTO.

INTRODUCTION

Stand Facing the River

WHENEVER I VISIT A TROUT STREAM, FLY FISHING EMPOWERS THE process. The sport's high technicians lean hard toward its empirical rewards, but I doubt that any of those admirable overachievers would be there in the first place if it wasn't all so beautiful. Fly fishing positions us so superbly to feel and wonder—abstractly, reverently, analytically, poetically, whimsically, or in any other way within our capabilities—that it would be a tragic loss of intellectual and emotional opportunity if the sport had never arisen as a human pursuit.[1]

When Roderick Haig-Brown made his famous remark that "perhaps fishing is, for me, only an excuse to be near rivers," he was right. But he knew, and meant, that the nearness of the river was only the start.[2] Pick up your fly rod, stand facing the river, and the world opens out from there.

In fact many worlds open from there. Some days, it's sufficient to think about where the fish might be, or why the flies aren't hatching, or why even the best fly tiers on earth can't seem to narrow down the appropriate pattern of the little western mayfly known as the Pale Morning Dun. Perhaps nothing else has so fully occupied fly fishers over the centuries than our quixotic and joyously addictive attempts to get a fly pattern right.

There are days when my inquiry may be, in the spirit of Haig-Brown, more about the river itself—changes in a once-familiar gravel bar since the last high water, a long bark-peeled snag that has been slowly creeping downstream through a favorite bend and now seems to have jammed itself permanently into a jutting angle of cutbank, or just an odd tint to the water that makes me wonder what has been going on upstream.

Other days, especially those when I go foraging in the folklore and literature of angling and the greater literatures of natural and human history, I am again struck by the open-ended character of the whole enterprise of outdoor sport, most especially the blessed uncertainty of it all. The combination of human nature and wild nature is always bound to be exciting, challenging, and a little bewildering.

For all these reasons, on all these levels, fly fishing is, as the phrase goes, "good to think with."[3] Fly fishing invites us into so many kinds of wonder and wondering that even in our most idle moods it can surprise us with new insights and questions. And if we really pay attention, we'll hardly keep up with all that's going on.

Fly fishing has changed more in the past century than in the previous two millennia, and it seems to be changing faster all the time. I suspect that most anglers and all of fly fishing's commercial enterprises would call this accelerating rate of change "progress," but it's probably also worth wondering if change necessarily makes a sport better. Technology, commerce, and human values play major roles here, and they are all up for grabs. *If Fish Could Scream* is a series of meditations on this process of change, but it's far less about how things are today than it is about how we got here.

In his fascinating book *Hunting and the American Imagination*, historian Daniel Herman describes how American sportsmen reinvented themselves in the latter half of the nineteenth century.[4] Before 1850 the game-hog/fish-hog "culture" prevailed and sportsmen were perceived as lazy ne'er-do-wells, shot at anything that moved, and wiped out fish and wildlife populations with no apparent awareness or remorse. But by 1900, under the leadership of Theodore Roosevelt, George Bird Grinnell, and their like, and backed by hundreds of newly created sportsmen's groups, American hunters and fishermen adopted a rational, forward-looking code of behavior, began to police themselves and train their children, and became widely respected not only as conservationists but as good citizens. Sportsmen, Herman persuasively argues, literally made themselves over, and by doing so not only changed the public's feelings about sport, but brought the wildlife back.

The novelty of this momentous transformation wasn't that sportsmen could change. As I will suggest many times in this book, everything about sport has typically changed in pace with its social, technological, and even biological contexts.[5] What is much more interesting about this particular change is how directed it seemed to be. Under the inspired leadership of the Roosevelts and the Grinnells, we picked ourselves up out of the social gutter and made ourselves into something we hadn't been before. We did this on purpose, both to ensure the future of our quarry and to improve our standing in the community.

We have changed more since then, including a continued refinement of the principles and values that drove Roosevelt and Grinnell. But most of the time we're not as intentional as Roosevelt and his pals were about where we're headed. We usually change in a haphazard way, and most of us don't give it much thought. Maybe we're just too distracted trying to come up with a decent PMD imitation. Whatever the reasons, I hope that this book reveals the extent to which fly fishing is poised for continued and probably accelerated change. I like to think that knowing change is coming, and being alert to its opportunities as well as to its risks, can be to our advantage.

The subjects of some chapters are intensely controversial among anglers today. "A Great Want of True Angling Sentiment" considers the competitive impulse among anglers, a hot topic because of the flourishing of amateur and professional fly-fishing contests, including a widely publicized fly-fishing world championship. Some participants in this debate invoke history and historic authorities to prove their cases for or against such contests, but our predecessors were no simpler or less quarrelsome than we are when it came to answering these questions. "Spinners and Sinners" traces the long rivalry between fly fishers and users of other kinds of tackle, a constant source of contention over fly fishing's perceived elitism. The title essay, "If Fish Could Scream," is about the supposed cruelty of anglers—a persistent criticism we have faced (or dodged) for several centuries. In an irony-rich examination of our reaction to this criticism, we find that our infamous self-perception as socially or even morally superior to other kinds of anglers originated in part because we once believed we were the least *cruel* of anglers. Now, because of our catch-and-release practices, we are seen by critics of sport fishing as the most cruel of all.

Other chapters consider matters that probably could use a little more controversy—or at least conversation—than they have generated so far. "Uncles and Other Heroes" explores the long-standing celebrity culture of fly fishing. The fly-fishing celebrity is not new, but the nature of the celebrated heroism has come a long way. "All the Long Desired Things," by focusing on the railroad boom of the nineteenth century, shows how transportation technology revolutionized fly fishing's engagement with the natural world. The typical fly fisher before 1800 rarely fished more than 25 miles from home, while today's angler has the whole world within reach. This change means that a lifelong, deep acquaintance with local water is often replaced by a cosmopolitan if shallow acquaintance with many waters. How unlike our ancestors does this make us? "If the Fishes Will Be Patient" is about the historic damming of every major American watershed and the effects of those dams on fly-fishing practice and values. The extraordinary popularity of dozens of newly created "tailwater" fisheries downstream from huge hydro dams has demonstrated the adaptability of the modern fly fisher, but these "new" rivers test the sport's environmental values in ways never before encountered. And "Outworn Privileges" visits one of the world's great and historic trout-fishing shrines and reminds us of how perilous our privileges as anglers can be in a rapidly changing world.

I realize that most casual anglers don't care much about these questions, but I know from my own travels in the world of fly fishing that many of us do take the sport's bigger issues seriously. Perhaps this book is for those who are already interested in such matters, but I can dream that others will also pick it up and begin to think harder about what we do out there on the water.

I also realize that I'm dabbling in a host of disciplines where my formal training is scanty. All of us with a scholarly specialty tend to get turfy when someone ambles in from a neighboring academic discipline and sets up shop in our backyard. I know I do; in my writings on environmental history I have often indignantly dumped on some ecologist (or, even worse, economist) who had the brass to act like a card-carrying historian. But interdisciplinary studies are the future for every form of scholarship related to natural resources, and we need to develop not only a greater tolerance for each other, but also a greater enthusiasm for working together. All of which is to say that I apologize in advance for any occasions upon which I may have carelessly (or incompetently) trod on the turf or toes of anthropologists, ethicists, folklorists, sociologists, ecologists, and any other specialists for whom fly fishing's complicated cultural saga is such a rich and inviting field of study. All I can say to you is: consider my shortcomings an invitation to take on these subjects yourself.

Fly fishing's debates and controversies are pretty much endless, and should be. We're better off for admitting that we will never completely sort these things out, and I'm not trying to win arguments here anyway. I certainly don't hide my own opinions, and now and then I do criticize some notion or belief that I find particularly feeble. But I hope that I have managed to offer this book in an open-ended spirit, one that might advance the conversations we require if we are to do justice to this wonder-filled sport, the natural world it relies upon, and the reinventions to come.

CHAPTER ONE

UNCLES AND OTHER HEROES

Fly Fishing and the Culture of Celebrity

MY FIRST FISHING HERO WAS MY UNCLE, RICHARD MURPHY. HE was a lifelong cane-pole baitfisherman and a fixture on his home lake in Ohio who enjoyed nearly seventy years of fishing experience. Funny thing is, aside from certain inadvertent lessons he gave me in the effective use of profanity, I would have a hard time describing even one specific thing he taught me about fishing.

It wasn't that Uncle Dick didn't teach me things. They just didn't matter as much as being out there with someone who had lived with the lake his whole life. Just hanging around with someone like that is exciting. There is great inspiration in the presence of genuine authority.

Many of us have been lucky enough to stumble into a situation where we could learn from some especially gifted angler. Every town has at least a few, and whether they're the upright souls who

The author's uncle, Richard Murphy (1916–1989), a longtime Ohio bait-angler, exemplified the venerable tradition of the local angling legend.
AUTHOR PHOTO.

patiently conduct fly-tying classes at the local school or the poachers whose license numbers are taped to the dashboard of every law enforcement officer in the county, they occupy a special place in our sport's culture. They represent some rare, admirable pinnacle of skill and experience. They know things the rest of us don't; they have seen things the rest of us can hardly imagine. They embody wisdom—or at least a backwoods craftiness that many of us would secretly prefer anyway.

THE NEED

We enjoy being in awe of someone like that. Whether we consider them role models or not, it feels good to know a genius. The experience of being star-struck is happily self-serving. There's a satisfying "if they could see me now" feeling in actually spending time with such a person. Many years ago, during my first conversation with Lee Wulff, one of the twentieth century's most influential anglers, I found it hard to listen to him because my brain kept shouting at me, "You're actually standing here in Lee Wulff's house having a conversation with Lee Wulff!"

There's more to it than that. Our fly-fishing heroes take care of things for us. They put in the hard years doing the homework on techniques, entomology, fly patterns, and all the other great technical questions. They pave the way into all sorts of arcane corners of the sport. They inspire us with their example and comfort us with their long, deep view of what the fly-fishing life means.

This is all especially important to the underachievers among us who have no intention of working as hard as the real experts have worked. We don't see them as role models as much as superathletes.[1] They reduce the pressure on us. We're happy just knowing that fishing can be practiced on such an exemplary plane. We don't need to mimic their exploits and triumphs. They've got the heroic end of the sport covered, and we can just bumble along feeling good about it. Having a hero, like being a hero, is not a simple thing.

Joseph Campbell, in his popular classic *The Hero with a Thousand Faces* (1949), described the ambivalence of the hero's image this way:

> The composite hero of the monomyth is a personage of exceptional gifts. Frequently he is honored by his society, frequently unrecognized or disdained. He and/or the world in which he finds himself suffers from a symbolical deficiency. In fairy tales this may be as slight as the lack of a certain golden ring, whereas in apocalyptic vision the physical and spiritual life of the whole earth can be represented as fallen, or on the point of falling, into ruin.[2]

None of this should sound unfamiliar to fishermen, from the exceptional gifts to the lack of recognition (or outright disdain). After all, only a few undistinguished people in my Uncle Dick's community realized or cared that they had a great master of an ancient craft among them. And as far as "symbolical deficiencies," just replace the mythic Golden Fleece or the Ring of Power with an equally mythic trout or a long-sought magical fly pattern, and we're talking about the same passionate intensity of purpose.[3] The difference is that in the case of fishing, only the fishermen care how it comes out, and the world isn't going to end if, as usual, we fail.

The cultural anthropologists might tell us that our hero-worshipping runs a lot deeper than our admiration for a few guys who can catch more fish than the rest of us. They might also remind us that not only did humans throughout history have an almost desperate need for heroes, but also that heroes are usually mythic.

But if the anthropologists were to look a little harder at us, they'd realize that we're way ahead of them. In our more lucid moments, we already know that fishing is a high quest thinly dis-guised as a sport. The trout is just another kind of grail. And in our hearts we knew all along that nobody could really be as good at catching fish as we like to believe our heroes are.

THE PROS

Before about 1800 or so, most of the heroes of the fly-fishing world were like my Uncle Dick—only locally famous. But some of them were actually professionals in the fishing business. As long ago as 1659, Londoner Thomas Barker wrote in his charming little book *Barker's Delight or The Art of Angling*, that "if you would have a rod to beare and to fit neatly, you must go to John Hobs who liveth at the sign of the George behind the Mews by Charing Crosse."[4] We might be tempted to say that Mr. Hobs and his contemporaries were that day's equivalents of Sage, Orvis, and other modern manufacturers. But because of the handwork involved in making any item of tackle so long ago, and because of these early tackle sellers' smaller output, they were probably more like the Pinky Gillums and Paul Youngs of their time—mid-twentieth-century artisans who built bamboo fly rods at a custom grade, for a small, select market—there was no large-scale tackle manufacturing back then.

But the point is still valid. It's a sure thing that seventeenth-century London's little tackle shops, as quaint as they might seem to us now, would have hosted the same gatherings of angling fanatics who find their way to modern tackle shops.

So when Charles Cotton, writing in the famous fifth edition of Walton's *Compleat Angler* (1676), praised his neighbor, Capt. Henry Jackson, as "by many degrees the best fly-maker I yet met with,"[5] he was telling us that the anglers of his time, like all others, paid full homage to the sport's cool hands.

But there are heroes on the one hand, and celebrities on the other. The blurry distinction between the two groups first began to matter to American fly fishers in 1829, when volume one of *The American Turf Register and Sporting Magazine* appeared. It was the first American periodical devoted entirely to sport, including horse racing ("the turf," as it was known), hunting, fishing, and other recreations, and in 1831 it was followed by the more successful *Spirit of the Times*, edited by William Trotter Porter.

I have written about Porter before, and still have hopes that he will eventually become more gratefully remembered.[6] He is the great forgotten hero of American fishing writing, the founder of American sporting journalism and the shaper of a publishing tradition that in some ways hasn't changed all that much in the ensuing

William Trotter Porter (1809–1858), now recognized as the father of American sporting journalism, was largely responsible for the creation of our first generation of sportsmen-celebrities in the years before the Civil War.

ILLUSTRATION BY MARSHA KARLE, FROM AN ENGRAVING IN FRANCIS BRINLEY, *LIFE OF WILLIAM T. PORTER* (1860).

years. In the *Spirit*, the *Turf Register* (which he later also owned), and a bibliographic tangle of other publications, he constantly celebrated leading anglers (or at least leading anglers who were also his buddies), thus promoting fly fishing over all other types of angling and creating our first generation of national angling celebrities.

By 1856, Porter claimed that his *Porter's Spirit of the Times*, the latest permutation of his commercial magazine adventures, was "backed by a circulation of 40,000 copies,"[7] a number that, if true (though I doubt it), would be enviable even among many specialty magazines today. Anglers, it seems, were anxious to hear from each other, to learn about the latest tackle, and to enjoy the exploits of their favorite heroes.

But that was only the beginning. A great proliferation of angling societies occurred after the American Civil War, with hundreds of rod and gun clubs popping up all over the country. Porter's pioneering journalism was magnified and enhanced tremendously in the 1870s and afterward, by great old periodicals such as *Forest and Stream* and *American Angler,* which fed the public's appetites for information, lore, and heroes with a whole new generation of popular writers, tackle makers, and other purveyors of angling essentials (such as the railroad travel described in the next chapter).[8]

THE UNCLES

The most beloved American angler of the nineteenth century, Thaddeus Norris, published his immense *The American Angler's Book* in 1864 and remained one of American angling's foremost heroes long after his death only thirteen years later. He was affectionately referred to by generations of readers as "Uncle Thad." It could even be argued that this special quality of uncle-hood was for a long time the most powerful element in angling celebrity.

Thaddeus "Uncle Thad" Norris (1811–1877) served as a surrogate long-distance "uncle figure" for generations of American anglers, even after his death.

ILLUSTRATION BY MARSHA KARLE,
BASED ON A PORTRAIT PUBLISHED IN
FRED MATHER, *MY ANGLING FRIENDS* (1901).

For many centuries before 1900, the overwhelming majority of fishermen learned their craft from a father, a brother, or a friend; no wonder that they gravitated toward the likes of a Walton or a Norris—elder-figure, self-reliant types who sat under trees smoking pipes and oozing gentle sentiments.

And no wonder that subsequent generations found their angling heroes among similar men. Two of the best-remembered of the twentieth century were Ray Bergman and Joe Brooks. Both Bergman and Brooks spent many years as fishing editor of *Outdoor Life*, and both—down-home, old-shoe writers of a practical bent—served as adopted long-distance uncles to generations of trout fishers.

In this respect, during the near-century between the death of Norris in 1877 and that of Brooks in 1972, fly fishing remained a pretty quiet pond. A deep-sea fisherman might make some headlines now and then, but the hero trade didn't bring a lot of glitz or even income to the life of fly fishing's famous and beloved.

THE MODERNS

But in the mid-1970s things seemed to change, abruptly and dramatically. Fly fishing grew in popularity, and in fashionableness. Suddenly, there were fly-fishing schools for all the people who'd missed out on uncle-instruction. An aggressively innovative high-tech tackle industry replaced the traditional organic components of fishing gear with ever more sophisticated synthetics. Dozens of upscale fly-fishing resorts, and hundreds of nice new fly shops sprang up. There was even a movie.

In a remarkably short period of time—the blink of an eye in the sport's thousands of years of history—the fly-fishing industry stepped out of the cottage. The fly-fishing community discovered

Joe Brooks (1905–1972), one of the twentieth century's most beloved fishing writers, was admired not only for his expertise but also for the comfortable accessibility of his writing—traits that placed him squarely in the Thaddeus Norris tradition. ILLUSTRATION BY MARSHA KARLE, FROM A PHOTOGRAPH COURTESY OF THE AMERICAN MUSEUM OF FLY FISHING, MANCHESTER, VERMONT.

the joys of conclaves, conventions, trade shows, and other gatherings. The professional uncles who were living out the honored last years of their careers found themselves keeping company with professors, technicians, philosophers, and poets. Fly fishing seemed to exemplify the evolutionary theory of punctuated equilibrium, skipping abruptly from one form to another. All the antes got upped at once.

The significance of this change first dawned on me around 1975 at a Federation of Fly Fishermen conclave in West Yellowstone, Montana. I was standing off to the side, listening in, as people waited in line to ask Dave Whitlock questions. I had already noticed that the conclaves involved a lot of hero-worship, as we took our turns to ask Dave, Doug Swisher, Enos Bradner, Ernest Schwiebert, or any of the other authorities a question or two about something they'd written, or some river they'd fished. Being one of the worshippers myself, I didn't see anything wrong with this except that I had to share the heroes with too many other people.

I'm still not sure what's wrong with it, but I date my unease about it to that moment, when a well-dressed older woman reached the front of Dave's line. Ever the gentleman, Dave greeted her with his usual cheerfulness. She told him that she didn't really have a question, she just wanted to compliment him on his hair.

Right there, for me, some line was crossed, and suddenly fly fishing wasn't just about fly fishing any more. Uncle Dick usually avoided talking to women, and his hair was unlikely to earn their admiration anyway.

THE STUFF OF HEROISM

It was only a few years later that Catskill fishing writer Art Lee began publicly referring to himself as a "professional fly fisherman," which apparently shocked a lot of people who preferred to think of fly fishing as the domain of gifted amateurs supported by a benign and entirely altruistic industry. But Art, one of our best writers, was just acknowledging what had always been true, that fly fishing, even for all the honorable types like Art, can also be about making a living.

William Porter and other prominent British and American sportsmen of his century understood the commerce of fame, and traded on it when they could. But, again, the recent changes have been striking.

In today's media-intense world, fly fishing's marketeers have successfully applied the same promotional devices to the sport as are applied to barbecue grills, luxury SUVs, and skin conditioners.

Endorsements are legion, and associations between leading angling authorities and tackle manufacturers are routine.

Most of us seem to enjoy all this, whether we see it as hype or genuine excitement. The flood of information and promotion sweeps over us, we paw through it at our leisure, and we grab what we like. It is infinitely easier today to become well-informed about fly fishing than it was even twenty years ago, and it is far easier to find just the right stuff to buy.

Buying stuff has always been a dicey part of fly fishing. We have long been counseled by the sport's graybeards that this isn't about ownership or greed, but about contentment and wonder. I agree with them and will return to this whole business of the sport's toys in chapter five. But let's face it: most of us do love "stuff." Fly fishers, perhaps more than most other sportsmen, are notorious for our accumulations of tackle, fly-tying materials, and related odds and ends. I distinctly remember a day about thirty years ago when my older brother Steve, who first involved me in fly fishing, was leafing through a brand-new fly-fishing book and jokingly said, "Where's the part where it tells me what to buy?" We knew that there was this involved relationship between the experts and the tackle companies, and we knew it complicated things, but we still wanted the experts to tell us what they thought we should buy. We joked about it all the time, how we appreciated the "retail therapy" and confidence-boosting effects of a few purchases on a slow fishing day, just to keep hope alive, and how we subscribed to the magazines for the ads rather than for the articles. Even with my extremely limited discretionary income, it was part of the fun.

Any number of commentators has pointed out the risks of replacing the sport with the stuff. I can invoke no higher authority on this matter than the great wildlife scientist, conservationist, and fly fisher Aldo Leopold, who, more than fifty years ago in *A Sand County Almanac* (1949), struggled with striking the right balance between technology and simplicity in our nature recreations:

> I do not pretend to know what is moderation, or where the line is between legitimate and illegitimate gadgets. It seems clear, though, that the origin of gadgets has much to do with their cultural effects. Homemade aids to sport or outdoor life often enhance, rather than destroy, the man-earth drama; he who kills a trout with his own fly has scored two coups, not one. I use many factory-made gadgets myself. Yet there must be some limit beyond which money-bought aids to sport destroy the cultural value of sport.[9]

Over the years, my fishing vest has bloated and slimmed cyclically, as I first declared my independence from excess and then succumbed, nifty gadget by nifty gadget, to it again. I doubt I'll ever find the perfect balance for my own "man-earth drama," but I still sense my own susceptibility when one of fly fishing's celebrities holds forth on this or that new miracle gizmo. I hardly ever buy these things any more, whatever they are, but I will never stop wondering, next time I'm getting skunked on some uncooperative stream, if maybe I should have. After all, an expert is an expert, and I'm not.

THE DURABLE HERO

I'm certainly neither the first nor only person to conclude that the establishment of what angling commentator Arnold Gingrich, writing in the 1970s, liked to refer to as a "pantheon" of experts, did eventually get a little over the top.[10] Like all sports, fly fishing attracts a variety of temperaments. For some, the solitude and the independence of spirit that seemed so essential in the angling tradition, at least as it was epitomized by the likes of Walton or Norris, has been trampled and discarded in the stockyards of the personality parades, big trade shows, fly-fishing conventions, and competitions. In this atmosphere, they feel, experts can be spontaneously generated, but heroes can't.

There's something to that. And yet I can't think of even one fly-fishing celebrity, and very few tackle manufacturers, who got seriously rich from it. The sport is just not that fertile a field. The pond is too small. Knowing what I do about the publishing of books, the giving of lectures, or the running of a fly shop, I know that in a narrow universe like fly fishing, those endeavors will be lucky to buy you a modest retirement bungalow, much less set you up in Beverly Hills. You might eventually make the cover of a fly-fishing magazine, but don't get your hopes up that *Newsweek* will notice. If you crave heroic status, you'd be better off to find another way to get it.

Now that I think about it, I realize that small-time anonymity was a part of my Uncle Dick's peculiar angling heroism. Years after my brother and I had grown up, left home, and settled in other states, we both happened to be in Ohio at the same time, and managed a day of fishing with Uncle Dick. The weather was miserable and there was no point in going out on the lake, so we all just messed around near the local marina, each engaged in that slow state of killing time while holding a fishing rod (or, in this case, a fishing pole).

After a while, my brother wandered over to the marina and started up a conversation with the guy who ran the place. Naturally, they talked about the fishing. To emphasize how lousy the fishing was right then, the marina guy pointed down the length of the docks to where Uncle Dick sat drowning another depressed worm, and said, "See that guy? That's Dick Murphy, and when he ain't catchin' 'em, *nobody's* catchin' 'em."

Suddenly, our own Uncle Dick—who had been a legend all along in our family for his fishing, his humor, his unique philosophy of life, and his stupendous belches—took on a whole new and glowing aspect for us. He was, we now realized, a cultural icon. He was a hero.

It seems to be a consensus among the observers I know that the great boom in fly fishing over the past thirty years has to an extent self-corrected some of its own early excesses. Our need for heroes didn't disappear, but it did recalibrate itself to cope with the sudden overabundance of candidates. As Arnold Gingrich's "pantheon" bloated with more and more Greats and Near-Greats, a reaction set in even among the most naively receptive of us and we ratcheted down our adulation. With so many legitimate experts out there, we didn't necessarily have to idolize all of them.

Our increasingly realistic view of fly fishing's celebrities might have been because of the volume of available information. When I stood in line in the 1970s to ask some famous fly fisher a question, it was because I didn't know of any other way to get the answer. Now, with thousands of websites providing relevant and up-to-the-second reports on travel, weather, tackle, accommodations, hatches, guiding, and water conditions for virtually every fishable water in the country, only the most dedicated, deep-digging specialists need ever stand in line again.

We might even wonder if this new saturation of information will do away with the need for the angling heroes we so admired only thirty or forty years ago. Even today, the sport's best-known figures, whether they are the aging stars of an earlier era or newcomers to the banquet circuit, don't seem to have quite the celebrity impact they did back then. We all know too much, and expertise is too readily achieved by the mere mortals among us to sustain the kind of worshipful mood that seemed so common a few decades ago.

We still need a few heroes, though, and not just to fill out the agendas at the hundreds of local, regional, and national conferences, conclaves, shows, and trade gatherings that require the focus of authority that these people provide. No matter that those most knowledgeable about rods, reels, flies, and all the rest of fly fishing's paraphernalia are for the most part the comparatively anonymous people who actually invent and manufacture those things. A quick cruise through the pages of most of the glossy fishing-tackle catalogs—whether fly fishing or not—will reveal the high marketing value placed on the famous fisherman's endorsement. The celebrity-authority is still the person we are most eager to listen to, no matter which manufacturer's payrolls got him to the show. Expertise needs a face. Authority is much more persuasive with a personality, a sense of humor, and a cheerful handshake.

In an important way, it appears that we've come full circle. As much as we enjoy knowing and reading about the far-off experts, I suspect that many of us are like Barker and Cotton, and are fundamentally local in our fishing. We read and dream of the big trips, but a lot of us mostly fish nearby, and it's nearby that we are best qualified to identify the great anglers among us anyway. Famous authors of famous books have their place, but when it comes right down to it, I want to know what Dick Murphy thinks.

Learning to fish from an older friend or relative has been one of fishing's most venerable and cherished traditions. Grandfather Leon Martuch coaches grandson Alan as he catches his first trout on a fly in a Montana spring creek. AUTHOR PHOTO.

Like Charles Cotton 350 years ago, we have learned that we don't really need to look beyond our own neighborhoods to find a good serviceable hero. For the purposes of our day-to-day fishing, we most need the gifted local fly fisher who catches fish when nobody else can, or tells the best stories, or in some other way draws us into the quiet heroism that we vaguely sense is, or should be, fundamental to the whole fly-fishing enterprise at its best.

CHAPTER TWO

ALL THE LONG-DESIRED THINGS

Trains, Tracks, and Trout

HERE IS ONE OF MY FAVORITE EARLY AMERICAN FISHING STORIES, a favorite for both what is good and what is bad in it. I mentioned it briefly in my book *Royal Coachman*, but I come back to it here because it so perfectly captures a day and a way of life that we can barely imagine—and a set of values we have long discarded.

Early one June morning in the 1820s, a party of five anglers in southern Vermont started fishing a favorite unnamed stream. Nine hours later, "with intervals, to cook and eat our breakfast and dinner, we had caught five hundred and seventy trout; more, indeed, than we could well carry back to our wagons." The jubilant writer telling this story in the *American Turf Register and Sporting Magazine* concluded that "it was a day's sport; such, I will venture to say, as was never known to Izaak Walton of old, that prince of anglers; and such as few of us will ever have the opportunity of enjoying again."[1]

What may be most amazing about statements like this is that these people, hauling big sacks of dead trout from the river, actually didn't seem to understand why the "opportunity" went away. But even in the presence of this swinish behavior, it might have been possible to find such amazing fishing in many remote parts of the lower forty-eight states for a very long time, if anglers had continued to rely on horses and foot travel to get there.

But they didn't. Railroads changed everything, and in a matter of a few decades the tracks chased those magical hog-heaven fishing opportunities across the continent and—except for a comparatively few wilderness areas and private reserves—right out of existence. We're still trying to put them back.

GETTING THERE

By the 1850s, trains were hauling eastern anglers to the edges of long-favored fishing grounds on Cape Cod and Long Island and even getting them close to newer fishing waters in the Poconos in Pennsylvania, the Catkills near New York City, and the Adirondacks of northern New York.[2] But it was the accelerating railroad boom after the war that took fishermen to so many regions that had been out of reach or even unheard of only a few years earlier.

The completion of the first transcontinental railroad in 1869 stands as a symbol of this great explosion of railroad building, and one man, William Henry Harrison Murray, likewise symbolizes the corresponding rush of sportsmen to the woods and waters at the receding edges of wilderness America. Murray achieved his peculiar immortality by writing a book, *Adventures in the Wilderness*, appropriately published in 1869 as well.[3] Murray's tales of fishing and camping struck an irresistible chord among city-bound sportsmen. His subject was the Adirondacks, and he almost single-

Through his articles, books, and speeches, Rev. William Henry Harrison Murray (1840–1904) was a major force in the rise of the American sportsman-tourist in the final decades of the nineteenth century.
ILLUSTRATION BY MARSHA KARLE, FROM A CONTEMPORARY ENGRAVING AND PHOTOGRAPH PUBLISHED IN A MODERN EDITION OF MURRAY'S *ADVENTURES IN THE WILDERNESS* (1989).

handedly turned the trickle of adventurous sportsmen visiting that wonderful region into a flood. Soon labeled "Murray's fools" and caricatured mercilessly in the popular press, these hordes not only crowded the lakes and streams, they initiated the cycle of development that always accompanies such attention—more people demand more services, which attract more people, and so on.

The growing crowds of recreationists did eventually inspire conservation efforts, of course. Those few sportsmen with sufficient means bought up choice areas to ensure for themselves a few untrampled lands and undepleted fisheries. Other people worked to set aside the great public park that protects so much of the Adirondacks today.

The same story repeated itself in every great sporting region across the country, and in every case trains get a lot of the blame—or credit—for a remarkably rapid transformation of the American sporting landscape. If you have any doubt about the thoroughness

The hordes of tourists who rushed to the Adirondacks following the publication of W. H. H. Murray's *Adventures in the Wilderness* (1869) were lampooned as "Murray's Fools." This caricature of them, from *Harper's New Monthly Magazine*, August 1870, shows them boarding a steamer, having just disembarked from the train in the background. The leader is presumably reading Murray's book.

of the railroad's influence, here is yet one more proof: The first person ever to propose in writing that Yellowstone be made a national park was not some high-minded pioneer conservationist or naturalist. It was an employee of the Northern Pacific Railroad named A. B. Nettleton.

RAILS AND RODS

This railroad revolution, with its dramatic effect on angling, was not just an American phenomenon. In 1857, British fishing expert William Stewart reported that "railway travelling has afforded the angler great facilities for the pursuit of his vocation. One, or at most two hours' ride, will convey all lovers of sport in any large town in Scotland to streams where there are plenty of trout; the North British Railway especially opening up from Edinburgh, in the Tweed and its tributaries, a field for angling unmatched in the kingdom; and of this advantage, to do them justice, anglers avail themselves to the utmost."[4]

The changes brought about by all these traveling anglers were both sizeable and complicated. In the 1870s, British railroads promoted their routes by selling "angler's concession tickets" that gave angling club members special rates.[5] This not only encouraged more fishermen to travel to distant fishing areas, it also led to an abrupt proliferation of new fishing clubs—and a far larger number of fishermen. The long-isolated salmon rivers of Scotland were suddenly easily reached, and here again easy access had complicated effects. Fishing fees skyrocketed, for one thing. But more interesting and subtle effects were felt at the same time. For example, the sudden influx of anglers from other regions swamped long-held local traditions of fly patterns, revolutionizing and homogenizing salmon-fly tying in the United Kingdom. Well-traveled anglers take their learning and preferences with them, and no angling region stays the same in the face of so much new information.

This sudden mobility among fishermen was the story all over England. David Webster began his odd, fascinating, and still helpful book, *The Angler and The Loop-Rod* (1885), by noting that "the forest of rods seen at our railway stations on a Queen's birthday or a bank holiday, might lead one to suppose that, if fishing be an art, there must indeed be many artists."[6]

In the United States, the railroads missed no opportunities to promote the fishing along their routes. By the 1880s and at least

For many centuries, anglers had fished mostly within a few miles of home, becoming intimately familiar with local waters. Railroads changed the sport by putting a great variety of distant waters within reach of many anglers.
ENGRAVING FROM HENRY WILLIAM HERBERT, *FRANK FORESTER'S FISH AND FISHING OF THE UNITED STATES* (1850).

for the next thirty years, railroads published advertisements, brochures, and even books raving about every little region's unique sporting opportunities. In prose at least as ecstatic and beckoning as the ads for any modern fishing lodge in any modern fly-fishing magazine, the railroads promised us heaven.

WHAT HAVE WE DONE?

What strikes us now about this vast frenzy of sporting tourism is the amazing quickness with which the glowing promotion of pristine fishing was replaced, among the fishermen at least, with grumpy nostalgia. For these fishermen, the good old days weren't long ago; they were just last year, before the crowds arrived. You really should have been here yesterday.

The conservation professional and popular fishing writer Robert Barnwell Roosevelt captured this changing mood well, describing his experiences fishing the fine small trout streams of the Catskills before, during, and after the flood of tourist anglers arrived by rail:

> The brooks of Long Island, especially on the southern shore, abound with trout. But they are few in comparison with the hordes that once swarmed in the streams of Sullivan and Orange counties, and in fact all the lower tier of counties in this State, before the Erie Railroad was built, and opened the land to the crowd of market men. I am proud to say that I have travelled that country when it took the stage coach twelve hours to go twenty-four miles, and when, if we were in a hurry, we walked, and sent our baggage by the coach. Now you are jerked along high above our favorite meadows, directly through our wildest hills, and often under our best streams, at the rate of forty miles an hour, and yet people call that an improvement. As well might you lug a man out of bed at night, and drag him a dozen times round his room, and fling him back into bed, and say he was improved by the

As early as the 1860s, popular angling writer Robert Barnwell Roosevelt mourned the replacement of the stagecoach's relaxed pace across the landscape with the faster railroads. "Barnwell," as he was known, complained that in traveling by rail he was "jerked along high above our favorite meadows, directly through our wildest hills, and often under our best streams, at the rate of forty miles an hour, and yet people call that an improvement."

ILLUSTRATION BY MARSHA KARLE, FROM A PHOTOGRAPH IN CHARLES HALLOCK, *AN ANGLER'S REMINISCENCES* (1913).

operation. No one wants to be lugged out of bed, precisely as no one wanted to travel beyond Sullivan County; the best shooting and fishing in the world was to be found there.

When the railroad was first opened, the country was literally overrun, and Bashe's Kill, Pine Kill, the Sandberg, the Mon Gaup and Callicoon, and even Beaver Kill, which we thought were inexhaustible, were fished out. For many years trout had almost ceased from out of the waters, but the horrible public, having their attention drawn to the Adirondacks, gave it a little rest, and now the fishing is good.

If you go there, stop at George Durrance's, in Wurtsborough, and if he boasts of fishing, as he will, ask him whether he remembers going to the Sandberg one day, many years ago, to show a Yorker how to catch trout.[7]

In his outstanding book, *The Battenkill* (1993), John Merwin pointed out that by 1856, when Manchester, Vermont, business-man Charles Orvis opened his rod-building shop, "the banner years of Battenkill brook trout were already long gone, and . . . after the Civil War the region's highly touted trout fishing became almost entirely dependent on hatchery fish."[8]

But hatchery fish were just what most anglers wanted. The problem was too many fishermen, all at once, killing too many fish. The answer, again and again, was not to control the fisher-men—it was to control the fish. And the best way these people knew to "fix" the fish-shortage problem was to add more fish, which they did with hatchery fish, whose transportation from the hatcheries to the streams was happily facilitated by—guess who?—the railroads.

In each region, those wonderful first fishing experiences, reported with such glee in the pages of *Forest and Stream, American Angler*, and many other periodicals, became a kind of baseline data set by which future fishing was to be judged.[9] Fisheries managers were somehow expected to match the incredible numbers experi-enced by those pioneer anglers. From coast to coast, the railroads made it practical to transport tremendous numbers of fish—both native and exotic—to the appropriate railheads for stocking, which led to enduring changes in the sport encountered by later anglers.

This isn't the place for yet another diatribe about the demo-niacal qualities of hatcheries, but it's worth pointing out that the early appearance of fish hatcheries on all these waters was in good part yet another testament to the power and reach of the railroads.

THE MOMENT

But let's set that troubling legacy aside for a moment. Let's think what it must have been like back then. Suddenly, after many centuries of anglers having no choice but to fish close to home, faraway waters were within their reach. In 1890, Emerson Hough, one of the original American sporting travel writers, wrote about some north-country lakes where "the bass were so thick you

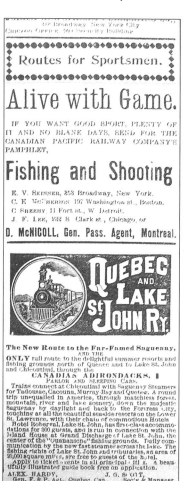

Following the American Civil War, recreation-hungry sportsmen comfortably rode the rails to formerly unreachable fishing and hunting grounds. As these ads from the August 18, 1894, issue of *Forest and Stream* show, railroads recognized sportsmen as an important market.

COURTESY OF JACK E. HAYNES COLLECTION, MONTANA STATE UNIVERSITY LIBRARY, BOZEMAN, MONTANA.

couldn't have pounded another one in with a hammer."[10] Who could read that wonderful hyperbole and not immediately start thinking of the train schedule to Wisconsin, Minnesota, or any of a hundred other dream destinations?

And even after the great railroad Fish Rush had ended and urban anglers everywhere had adopted favorite waters far from town, who cannot appreciate the giddy anticipation of Viscount Grey of Falloden, whose hectic London political career was punctuated with happy weekend retreats to the already-revered southern British chalkstreams? Writing in 1899, he exulted that after a few hours' trip, "you step out of the train, and are in a few minutes among all the long-desired things. Every sense is alert and every scent and everything seen or heard is noted with delight. You are grateful for the grass on which you walk, even for the soft country dust about your feet."[11]

This, for good or ill, is what the trains gave us. Cars and planes eventually gave it to us even more swiftly and thoroughly. But the trains first made many fishermen such wanderers, and led us into the double lives so many of us now live—town-bound and daydreaming most of the time, but free to cast our lines on some beloved distant river the rest.

HOME WATERS

What this accelerated ease of travel has meant to fly fishing—or any other sport, for that matter—is probably worth a lot more thought than we've given it. In previous books I have ruminated on the difference between the local, who lives on or very near a trout stream, and the "city fisherman," who visits it now and then.[12] Though I used to fancy myself a local fisherman and succumbed to the easy condescension locals smugly apply to the tourists, I have concluded that neither local nor city angler is on any particular high road compared to the other. Too many locals, I've noticed, tend to take the blessings of a trout stream for granted for the very reason that it's just part of their everyday life. The city fisherman treasures every second on the water and every sight of every pool. Both groups bring their own sensitivities, strengths, and weaknesses to the place. Every river is going to need all these friends tomorrow even more than it does today.

But I do share a concern I've heard from others, about the detachment bred from only having those brief if brilliant encounters with a stream or lake, no matter how much we cherish it and daydream about it the rest of the year. My fear is that those far-distant fishermen will find the rare encounters with expensive rivers to be enough; that they will compartmentalize their lives so comprehensively that they convince themselves that for the rest of the year it's okay to get along without.

That is an error. It is not okay. Wonder is not a hobby. The restorative glories of nature aren't just some injection we make an appointment for when we finally can't keep up with the rest of the rats. Wonder is a fundamental element of a healthy life.

I come to this concern because I've seen the same problem in action during my long involvement with national parks. National parks preserve representative examples of the wonder and power of the North American landscape before we similarly abandoned it to the rats. Thank heavens for the parks; so much of our cultural and natural heritage would be completely, instead of mostly, lost without them. Wherever we live, we should indeed go to these places, just as every serious fly fisher should hope to make a few pilgrimages to the faraway waters that fuel our sport's grand folklore. But treating nature respectfully in national parks and similar preserves can too easily become a salve for the conscience—a kind of perverse permission to treat nature disrespectfully everywhere else.

Fly fishing, like all other sports for almost all other people, was a neighborhood activity for almost all of its history. Just as our heroes were mostly local, so were our streams and our fish. It's hard to overstate the difference between the fly fisher of 200 (or 2,000) years ago and today's airborne anglers in this respect. Growing up along the streams we fished made us deeply familiar with them. Perhaps it made us narrow, too, but let's keep in mind that many of our greatest known angling authorities were people who made their discoveries and found their wisdom near home by fishing deeply in every sense of the word. If you're paying attention, you don't grow narrow; you just grow.

It's also true, to further complicate the deliberation, that most of fly fishing's famous authorities over the past several centuries may not have fished far from home but they "traveled" by reading anything they could get their hands on about fishing in other places. The great historical fly-fishing conversation that I have celebrated in previous books was, in that sense, an early surrogate for the train.

But going far away to fish, especially over a lifetime of such trips, also has its advantages. Technically, it exposes you to more kinds of fishing, which, with a little luck, will make you more skilled. Experientially, it exposes you to more kinds of *thinking* about fishing, which, with a little luck, will make you wiser. If you're paying attention in the midst of this luxurious travel regimen, you don't grow jaded; you just grow.

We will have both kinds of fishermen now, and I wonder if the ease of travel doesn't in some way entitle the city fisherman, at least the one who returns to a chosen faraway stream again and again faithfully for many years, to begin to think of such a remote place, though it be thousands of miles from his house, as his home river. I'm sure many traveling anglers feel that way, just as I suspect others feel that it's to our advantage, and to the advantage of the rivers, for us to fall in love with as many rivers as we can.

Still, planes, trains, and automobiles have changed us and have made things that were once difficult or impossible very easy. From the time of the construction of the first railroads, many modern fly fishers embraced improvements in travel technology as eagerly as we seem to embrace every other new thing that comes along. Others, even some who could afford to go, stayed home anyway, finding the fulfillment they needed without the trip.

I may sometimes have envied the travelers who saw all those wonderful new places, and on my own modest continental scale I made many of the same pilgrimages. I still do, now and then.

But in the long haul I guess I admire the stay-at-homes more. It's an entirely personal, largely subjective choice. I know a tourist from a local, and I've always preferred to be a local. If I can't find all the long-desired things close to home, either I'm living in the wrong place or they don't exist anyway.

CHAPTER THREE

SPINNERS AND SINNERS

I DATE THE PERCEPTION OF MYSELF AS A SERIOUS FISHERMAN TO A little more than forty years ago, when I acquired a Garcia Mitchell 300 spinning reel, which I saw and still see as fishing tackle's entry into that small group of "classic" types of machines and instruments—the 1957 Chevy, the Smith and Wesson Model 19 revolver, the Martin D-28 guitar, and the IBM Correcting Selectric typewriter all come to mind—that serve as gold standards in their respective fields.

One thing I didn't understand, however, is what "spinning" meant. I assumed it had something to do with the reel, probably with the perfect smoothness with which the monofilament line flowed off and on the spool, or with the spinning-wheel precision of the mechanism itself. The Mitchell was, after all, a great

In the early decades of the American popularity of spinning, the Garcia Mitchell 300 was one of the reels to achieve—as this advertisement put it—"hallmark of quality" status.

FROM THE 1961 *GARCIA FISHING ANNUAL*, COURTESY OF THE AMERICAN MUSEUM OF FLY FISHING, MANCHESTER, VERMONT.

mechanical idea at the height of its powers, and there was a spider-fiber sort of magic to its operation.

That I could own and "spin-fish" with such a reel for years, and now and then go out and buy a few Mepps spinners without noticing their name or thinking much about what it might mean, indicates a certain dull blitheness, I know, but it also suggests that I was, like a lot of fishermen, preoccupied with results rather than nomenclature. Besides, I was so charmed by the spinning reel itself that there seemed no need to look beyond its smooth, beautiful engineering to justify its name. Though I have examined some of the finest, most universally adored fly reels in history (you haven't lived until you've seen the rare gold-plated model of the Orvis 1874 reel), I have yet to see any fly reel that approaches the Garcia Mitchell 300 for pure mechanical satisfaction.

FLIGHTS AND WITCHES

But, in fact, in the sport of "spin" fishing, we're actually talking about the lure. For centuries, anglers have been making lures spin, turn, and flash in the water. In the 1600s, Izaak Walton himself gave us a careful discussion of how to mount a dead minnow on a big hook with its tail bent "a little to the right or left hand" so that it will "turn quick in the water . . . it is impossible that it should turn too quick."[1]

For centuries, "spinning" had nothing to do with the reel. One could and did fish a "spinner" with whatever tackle was at hand, from the most sophisticated to the crudest. It was all about getting the minnow (real or artificial—both were in common use by 1800) out into the current and forcing it against that current fast enough so that it would work its magic. In a spooky reverse parallel to dry-fly theory, just as generations of fly fishers incorrectly claimed that you couldn't fish a dry fly downstream, generations of spin fishers said you couldn't spin a lure by casting it upstream.

Fly-pattern innovators have had nothing on the spinning crowd. Nineteenth-century anglers developed a hardware store–full of patent-office candidates in their efforts to perfect spinning. Book after book and catalog after catalog portrayed an endless variety of vaguely medieval-looking wire-and-hook contrivances (variously known as flights, sets, and rigs) that consisted mainly of a

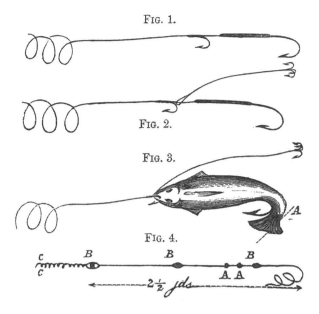

Sir Randal Roberts, in *The River's Side; or, The Trout and Grayling, and How to Take Them* (1866), illustrated basic spinning rigs similar to those advocated at least since Walton's time. Notice that the baitfish's tail was intentionally bent to one side to create the necessary spinning effect. COURTESY OF THE TROUT AND SALMONIDS COLLECTION, MONTANA STATE UNIVERSITY, BOZEMAN, MONTANA.

central metal shaft (often of shaped lead) from which hung a fearsome array of single, double, or treble hooks. By any of a variety of means, a dead minnow was attached to the shaft, and the thing was ready to use. Hewitt Wheatley's "Water Witches," his artificial minnows illustrated in *The Rod and Line: Or, Practical Hints and Dainty Devices for the Sure Taking of Trout, Grayling, Etc.* (1849), featured as many as fifteen hooks. Dainty devices indeed.[2]

One intriguing difference between many of these Victorian–era spinners and later lures was that in some cases the hooks were not directly attached to the lure itself. Instead, external lines, like outriggers, extended freely along the flanks of the real or fake fish,

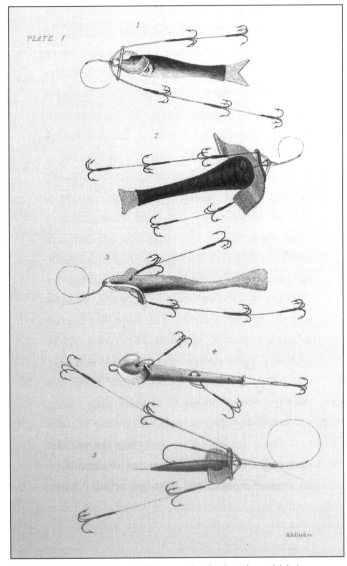

Hewitt Wheatley's formidably armed spinning rigs, which he referred to as "water witches," suggest the proficiency of the mid-nineteenth century British spin fisher. FROM HEWITT WHEATLEY, *THE ROD AND LINE* (1849).

and treble hooks were strung in series along these lines. Some writers called these hooked lines "drags." The idea was that a fish that grabbed the lure but failed to inhale the whole package would very likely be snagged around the mouth, eyes, or head by these free-swinging gangs of hooks. This style of spinner probably faded from fashion partly because it must have been a mess to handle, especially when trying to land a frantically struggling fish, and partly because the sporting definition of a fair-caught fish has evolved to exclude hooking the fish outside its mouth.

Another difference between these earlier spinners and today's models is that the swivel—the little free-spinning metal connection that allowed the lure to turn without the line getting all twisted up on itself—was usually placed not at the head of the lure but some distance up the line. William Stewart, in his strongly opinioned *The Practical Angler* (1857), recommended that one swivel "should be placed about two feet above the hook, and a second about a yard farther up."[3] This separation of swivel and spinner is intriguing, and probably worked just fine, but I suppose it faded from use because anglers preferred the simpler arrangement of the lure and swivel as part of the same dainty device.[4]

Through the nineteenth and early twentieth centuries, both British and American tackle manufacturers expanded the number of spinnable lures beyond all hope of counting. With the American development of excellent casting reels before the Civil War, it became possible to pitch hefty lures great distances with extraordinary accuracy. Many of those lures featured propellers, angled fins, and other clever attachments designed to heighten their rotation and attraction. Lighter, miniaturized versions of many of these same designs were marketed for use with fly rods, and they remained popular for much of the twentieth century. One of the most famous brown trout in more than two centuries of Pennsylvania fishing lore—and for many years the state record—was a fifteen-and-a-half-pound fish taken in 1945 by Don Martin of Fort Hunter. He caught the fish from Big Spring, near Carlisle, using a bamboo fly rod to cast a #12 Strawman Nymph with a 4/0 Colorado Spinner at its head.[5]

REAL SPINNING REELS

Though historical commentators have pointed out that the principles of the modern spinning reel were worked out by a variety of people in England, Scotland, Switzerland, and probably other places, British inventor Alfred Holden Illingworth developed and popularized the first ones we'd recognize, shortly after the First World War. Ironically, unlike fly reels and casting reels, whose spools actually do spin, the spinning reel relies on a fixed spool, aimed axis-forward so that the line practically melts off it when the lure is cast. This frictionless dispensing of the line was a huge advantage over traditional casting reels, whose line had to be dragged from the rapidly turning spool by the cast lure, with the constant threat of backlash. Combined with progressively better nylon lines, spinning reels enabled generations of post–World War II anglers to make long, accurate casts after only a little practice. It was a revolution, and not a quiet one.[6]

Though Bache-Brown Luxor spinning reels were first imported to the United States from England in about 1935, it wasn't until after World War II that a variety of reels arrived here in such numbers as to change the way Americans fished. The good reels were still comparatively cheap, they were amazingly easy to learn, and they landed in the New World right in the middle of the greatest recreation boom in American History, as millions of people—many of whom were new to fishing of any kind—hit the streams with more leisure time than ever.

This was a far more widespread change in fishing than the dramatic increase in fly fishing in the 1970s—this was a whole country hooked on a new sport. Some of the nation's leading outdoor writers, including such rising household fly-fishing names as Joe Bates and A. J. McClane, jumped on the popularization bandwagon and wrote books extolling and explaining the new gear.[7]

Many anglers considered spinning as the welcome bridge over an imagined gap between the lightest flies and lures that could be cast with fly rods and the heavy lures that could be cast with traditional casting rods and reels, although it wasn't that simple. It certainly was true that spinning gear could cast lures lighter than most traditional casting rigs could handle, but there were plenty of fly rods sturdy enough to cast small lures, too. As well, spinning outfits were soon available that could cast very heavy lures. Alert American tackle dealers realized this; Orvis adopted the Pelican spinning reel, made in Italy, renamed it the Orvis 100, and marketed it into the first widely used saltwater spinning reel.[8]

Spinning's real advantages were its ease and cheapness. Charley Waterman, in his wonderfully down-to-earth *A History of Angling* (1981), emphasized the cheapness:

> When spinning really got going in the late 40s, it came with a few high-grade reels and some appalling junk.
>
> The junk came because builders and importers saw that a great many new fishermen were going to get spinning gear and that the market was going to depend on price. Many were what tackle dealers called "throw away" outfits, intended to last for one fishing trip, and sometimes

they didn't even do that. One importer exhibited a boxful of Japanese imports, all different. He said they cost him roughly a dollar apiece in this country and he wondered which would be the best one for his line.[9]

THE OPPOSITION

It was also Charley who best summed up the anti-spinning reaction among traditionalists:

The spinning thing got silly in the early 50s when some of its opponents announced that it meant the death of all other forms of casting and that it might be necessary to pass new laws to keep it from completely wiping out fish populations.[10]

Spinning's "opponents" weren't lightweights. They included Edward Ringwood Hewitt, now an ancient and venerated grand old man of fly fishing, whose long life in the sport yielded so many influential books and ideas. Interviewed in 1957, just before his death, Hewitt ranted against the deadly efficiency of "this whole spinning business," and insisted that all state fish and game agencies should outlaw it.[11] There was an almost moral indignation here, as if spin fishers weren't really fishermen at all, but some vile new kind of social scum.

While spinning didn't lead to Trout Armageddon, there is no question that the great increase in the number of fishermen, their choice of tackle notwithstanding, was hard on the available fisheries.

On the other hand, by all accounts one serious effect of spinning's popularity was a corresponding eclipse in fly fishing. Never all that large a portion of the fishing population, fly fishers found themselves dwindling and left behind.

An interesting measure of this decline in fly fishing may be seen in the appearance of several excellent, even path-breaking fly-fishing books, including Art Flick's *Streamside Guide to Naturals and Their Imitations* (1947), Vincent Marinaro's *A Modern Dry-Fly Code* (1950), John Atherton's *The Fly and The Fish* (1951), and several others. A few of these (such as Ernest Schwiebert's uniquely broad *Matching the Hatch*, published in 1955 and offering fly fishers their first nationwide overview of trout-stream insects) seem to have flourished, but most sold slowly and didn't become prominent and influential "classics" until the 1970s, when they were resurrected by Nick Lyons and introduced to new generations of anglers, who made some of them into bestsellers.[12] Flick, Marinaro, and the others had labored on their information and theories for many years before spinning arrived, but just happened to release their studies in book form at the wrong time, when there was the least interest in new fly-fishing thinking. Who needed to know about bugs and new fly patterns when there were all these shiny little metal doodads that the trout just couldn't resist?

Eventually fly fishing climbed out of its market pit and re-established its prominence among the different kinds of angling. In a thoughtful essay, "Sinning Against Spinning," published in *Trout Madness* (1960), Robert Traver chronicled his own conversion from fly fishing to spinning and his eventual reversion to the fly rod. Charmed like so many others by the amazing efficiency of good spinning tackle, Traver announced it "the new love of my life," but got over it very quickly.

With my customary childish curiosity and helpless compulsion to possess every new fishing gadget that comes along, I too fell for spinning—hook, line, and sinker. Some two-hundred-dollars-worth-of-equipment later I woke up, rubbed my eyes, and decided that I did not give a tinker's damn for this new method of taking trout. In fact I gave up spinning before many fishermen in these parts had even heard of it, and instead returned to my fly fishing with, if possible, an even greater sense of joy and dedication. . . . It is not so much that I hate spinning, but rather that I love fly fishing so much better.[13]

The irresistibly quotable Traver gave us a list of the reasons why so many converts to spinning eventually drifted back to flies. Some reasons were quite practical, such as his dislike of taking so much time to retrieve the line for the next cast; he could lift his fished-out fly line from the water and recast it at any time, all at once. Other reasons were more subjective and, ultimately, more important:

But none of these objections goes to the heart of the matter and I suspect that I would still prefer to fly fish for trout with the conventional split bamboo fly rod and regular tapered silk or nylon line even if all the technical objections to spinning were solved. I rather think that the simplest statement is that I find the art and ritual of fly casting a joyous and poetic experience in itself, fish or no fish. Perhaps it is sheer sentimentality or conservatism on my part; perhaps it is a stubborn desire to do things the hard way; but somehow or other I like and prefer the sense of *personal involvement* and *immediacy* and *control* that I, at least, feel only when I am delicately casting my fly over likely trout waters.[14]

The purism of fly fishing is usually portrayed as a kind of snobbery, and sometimes it is. But in this one paragraph Traver captured the finer essence of the purist's heart.

GETTING ALONG FOR GREATER GOOD

Spinning came along as American angling entered its most dynamic and restless decades. More was going on than a flood of new tackle. Anglers were joining the real world, becoming conservation activists in unprecedented numbers. Trout fishermen particularly were finding a voice and flexing political muscles, most

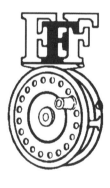

The two conservation organizations most closely associated with fly fishing, the Federation of Fly Fishers (originally the Federation of Fly Fishermen) and Trout Unlimited, differed fundamentally—FFF focusing on a certain type of tackle and TU focusing on certain fish species. Happily, the two groups routinely cooperate on many types of projects on both the local and national levels. COURTESY OF THE AMERICAN MUSEUM OF FLY FISHING, MANCHESTER, VERMONT.

often through the offices of Trout Unlimited, founded in 1959, and the Federation of Fly Fishermen (later the Federation of Fly Fishers) founded in 1965. Because many of the founders and early members of both these organizations were primarily interested in fly fishing for trout, there was a period in the late 1960s and early 1970s when serious conversations took place about simply combining these two into one more powerful group.[15]

The merger never happened, and it's easy enough to argue that there were good reasons. Starting in the 1950s, a tremendous broadening of interest among fly fishers led them to a great variety of fresh- and saltwater fish that, though many had been caught on flies long before, had never been of wide interest. The FFF was, by its own definition, not just about trout. It was about the expansion of the sportsman's horizons to include dozens of other fish species and fishing opportunities.

TU, on the other hand, prided itself on a different kind of breadth, across the spectrum of trout-fishing methods from bait to spinning lures to flies. The all-encompassing democracy of TU's approach, based in a desire to attract the largest possible constituency to the cause of trout conservation, was not something to be tossed aside lightly.

There were also a number of philosophical differences between the groups, including the centralized authority of TU and the grassroots approach of the FFF. But for the moment let's consider not the political animal at one end of the fishing line, but the hook at the other. The fish-hooking dilemma for TU, as was often pointed out to them, was how hopelessly anti-conservation some trout-fishing methods were. While both TU and FFF promoted limiting your kill and some forms of catch-and-release, even in the 1960s many people realized that bait-caught fish suf-

Arnold Gingrich, author of several congenial fly-fishing books in the 1960s and 1970s, was an advocate for the Federation of Fly Fishers and Trout Unlimited merging into one presumably more powerful organization.
ILLUSTRATION BY MARSHA KARLE FROM A PHOTOGRAPH IN THE ARNOLD GINGRICH COLLECTION OF THE BENTLEY HISTORICAL LIBRARY, UNIVERSITY OF MICHIGAN, ANN ARBOR, MICHIGAN.

fered a far higher release mortality than did fly- or lure-caught fish. Releasing dead fish seemed to miss the point. FFF leaders saw no reason to dilute the effectiveness of fly fishing as a catch-and-release tool by inviting bait fishers into the fold.

Neither TU nor the FFF was willing to give on this matter. Fly-fishing commentator Arnold Gingrich, ruminating somewhat grumpily over this problem in *The Joys of Trout* (1973), said, "But while TU refuses to abandon bait, just as stubbornly as the fly fishermen refuse to compromise their identity, which they equate with their integrity, the situation shows all the earmarks of an impasse—which is something that goes forward steadily backward."[16]

Over the succeeding years, TU may never have abandoned their hopes of attracting the bait fishers into their ranks (not that they give them much room in their beautiful magazine). The two organizations have gone their separate but overlapping ways.

Meanwhile, out on the streams, many of both organizations' clubs and chapters either acquired joint affiliations or otherwise cooperated in the good work. The barriers between the FFF and TU may have been organizationally insurmountable but were otherwise full of holes. Twice now, one individual has held a key administrative position first with TU and later with the FFF. Esther Simon was the first to accomplish this, in the 1980s, and Pete Van Gytenbeek, an early TU executive director, became FFF's president in 2004.

Crossing the boundary seemed the only way to do both jobs. As Gingrich put it, with an almost audible shrug of resignation, "Well, since they're both on the side of the angels, there's obviously only one thing to do. You've got to join them both, and keep your fingers crossed."[17] Which is just what many of us have done, for a couple generations now.

If the TU-FFF story seems like a tangential aside, consider this. Behind all this political history is one consistent if often unspoken element in the story of these two essential organizations' inability to work together even more closely. Most of the time, the issues that kept them apart lined up people with fly rods on one side and people with spinning rods on the other.

THE SOCIAL GAPS

When I became involved in fly fishing in the early 1970s, there was a formidable body of opinion among fly fishers that their method was superior, not merely in Traver's sense of providing a finer personal experience, but as a means of conserving hard-used fish populations. I remember pointing out to people with this view that science suggested otherwise—that fly fishing was no less harmful in catch-and-release fisheries than certain types of spin fishing. Some of those people didn't want to hear it. They believed in scientific management only until science ran up against their prejudices.

The statistics have accumulated overwhelmingly since then. We fly fishers may pride ourselves on occupying some aesthetic or even spiritual high ground among anglers if we want to, but that's about all we can pretend to have going for us any more. Spin fishers can release just as many fish alive as we can, if they wish to. Ed Hewitt would hate to hear that, and would probably burst out with, "But they don't wish to! They'll kill them all!" And I do know spin fishers who are just like that. But if we don't like them as people, or if we disapprove of their attitudes and values, let's not waste time taking it out on their tackle.

If I were still an active spin fisher, I'd cast a jaundiced and jealous eye on fly-fishing-only waters around the country, and wonder loudly how come those guys are getting these private little fishing reserves of their own on public streams that are managed mostly by tax dollars. But I also hope that I would listen with some sympathy to the less scientific justifications for such fly-fishing-only waters.

For one thing, there is something to the argument that some types of fishing simply require a little water of their own. The total fly-fishing-only stream mileage is trivial nationally; surely we are rich enough in aquatic resources that we don't have to subject all waters to the tragedy of the commons.

Also, there are a great many more "special-regulations" waters (almost always catch-and-release, or at least a restrictive slot limit) that do allow both fly- and spin-fishing but exclude bait fishing because of its high release mortality. Fly fishers and spin fishers seem to get along okay there, though in the places I know that have such regulations, the fly fishers tend to dominate the local fishing population, just because so many more of them have no interest in taking fish home anyway.

Last, there is the imponderable matter of tradition. Fly fishers perceive some of their most historic waters almost as shrines. For generations, sometimes for more than a century, fly fishers have devoted enormous amounts of energy and money to protect and nurture those particular waters. Eloquent books have brought literary immortality to a number of these places, in fact have defined them as places in regional culture. Most of the cultural aura of such places—everything from the local place names to the quirky local service businesses—is a product of the long-present society of fly fishers. Surely, that should earn them a little preference here and there.

SEPARATE BUT EQUAL ... ISH

There are chicken-or-egg questions here. Do fly reels and spinning reels attract different classes of people on some level of intellect or temperament, or are different kinds of people just using fly fishing and spin fishing as social badges, to distinguish themselves from each other? Do we fly fish because we don't like to spin fish, or vice versa? My own best answer to these questions is, "Maybe not, but sometimes it looks like it."

There are many spinning lures that I could comfortably cast with my fly rods (I know this from early experience, when I was still switching over). There are quite a few Woolly Buggers, Montana Nymphs, and other large-caliber flies in my vest that I could comfortably cast with a light spinning outfit. With a small plastic bubble a couple feet up the line, the lightest small flies can be cast, somewhat imprecisely, with a spinning rod. The boundaries between the hook-delivery capacity of the two methods are so blurred that an uninformed but perceptive observer might wonder what the fuss is about.

I have wondered myself. At my most dispassionate, driving along some favorite river, I see the passing ranks of fly fishers decked out in our generously flapped/pocketed/velcroed layers of fashionable pastels and breathable earth tones, and I wonder if even the most outlandishly dressed golfer could look any foppishly sillier to the uninitiated.

Then I see a spin fisher in faded jeans (the People's pastel) and flannel shirt standing (they never crouch like we do) with his toes right up to the edge of some beautiful trout stream, and I am reminded of Russ Chatham's description of such a man, "flipping a spoon carelessly into the water the way another might discard a candy wrapper."[18] Then I wonder if I looked that emotionally remote from what I was doing when I was a spin fisher.

Though I have many recollections of myself and others in ridiculous, embarrassing, and foolish situations while fly fishing, my strongest memory of any fisherman achieving the highest level of disconnection from actual fishing did happen to involve a spin fisherman. It was more than twenty years ago, in Vermont. I had stopped at the Union Street bridge over the Battenkill, not far downstream from Manchester, just to take a look at the water, which was low and clear. It was also very pretty, so I stood for a little while in the middle of the bridge, looking upstream. Unlike many other "bridge pools," this was unpromising water, just a couple inches deep over a bright bed of sand and gravel.

But on the west bank just upstream from the bridge there was some bare dirt right down to the water, and a local young man had parked his big pickup truck so he and his girlfriend could walk down and sit close together by the water while he fished. He had a nice spinning outfit and had cast out thirty feet or so, into the middle of the river. I looked down and watched his shiny little spinner as the clear current slowly rolled it along over the gravel in the ankle-deep water.

It was a telling moment. He knew essentially nothing about what a spinner was supposed to do or where to do it, and yet he was picturesquely honoring all the forms of "going fishing." It was a *Tableau vivant* of the Young Angler's Idyll. The disconnect between really fishing and what this young man was doing was stupendous, but I recognized immediately that this, too, was a kind of fishing, though it wouldn't produce an actual fish if he did it for a thousand years.

I also sensed a rare achievement here. For all the quixotic casts I've seen fly fishers make—including deranged long shots I've sent under logs, over weed beds, between branches, and into other sure tippet-clippers—I've never seen anyone approach this happy young fellow for sheer purity of hopelessness. It makes me think better of spin fishers generally to know that they, like us, can get so lost in the idea of fishing that catching a fish no longer matters.

GETTING ALONG AFTER ALL

Fishermen have always enjoyed poking fun at one another, and probably always will; it's just human nature, and it's often done in a friendly enough spirit. It would take a herd of sociologists—and maybe a few psychologists—to unravel the relationship between modern spin fishers and fly fishers. Spin fishers who puff up and blather on about how they can outfish fly fishers ought to just get on over to the fish market and stop taking up valuable river space. And anyone who has taken up fly fishing for some pathetic sense of superiority it gives them has bigger problems than fishing can solve.

Generations of fly-fishing writers have referred to bait-, lure-, or spin-fishing as stages of angling they passed through before "graduating" to fly fishing. But many of fly fishing's greatest authorities did not differentiate among fishing methods so condescendingly. Francis Francis (1822–1886) was for more than a quarter of a century the editor of the leading British periodical of sport and country life, *The Field*. Francis was both a prominent fly-fishing authority and a lifelong practitioner of worm fishing, which he celebrated for its "solitude and self-communing among scenes that tell no lies and brook none."

ILLUSTRATION BY MARSHA KARLE FROM AN ENGRAVING IN FRANCIS'S *A BOOK ON ANGLING* (1867).

I find it reassuring that many of the angling authorities who fished spinners a century or more ago were also leading fly-fishing authorities. Such great and beloved generalists as our own Uncle Thad Norris and the British writer Francis Francis did it all. In the twentieth century, some of our most popular fly-fishing writers, including Ray Bergman, Joe Brooks, and A. J. McClane, were also avid spin fishers. That's good enough company for me.

I suspect that many of us who started with a spinning outfit have never entirely escaped its charms. Like Robert Traver, I fly fish because I like it better. But I still take that old Mitchell out now and then, give the crank a few wistful turns, and consider my options.

CHAPTER FOUR

A GREAT WANT OF TRUE ANGLING SENTIMENT

Is Competitive Fly Fishing Fatal?

COMPETITION—AND ITS IMPLIED COMPANION, AGGRESSION—HAS been the subject of countless scientific and popular commentaries, in which we humans are likened to, distinguished from, or merely informed about the competitive urges of many other species of animal. Like love, competition has many admirers and more than a few detractors. Competition, we are told, is the creator of fitness—as individuals, as mates, as communities, as markets, as corporations, as teams, as schools, as nations, as races. Competition is the driver of progress, the breaker of hearts, the maker of champions, the meaning of life. No wonder we talk, write, and think about it so much. It is an inordinately complex matter. Whether or not each of us decides to believe that it is an inherent or essential part of human nature, it is an undeniably important part of modern human life.

Competition in sport has likewise been through the critical and popular opinion mills. For some commentators, competitive sports have been seen as society's safety valve, giving us a way to let off aggressive steam that would otherwise increase the murder rate and overpopulate the jails. For others, those same competitive sports are the training grounds of citizenship, teaching us to honor a hundred locker-room banners about teamwork, being tough and getting going, and getting along. For others, competitive sports are spectacles and pageantry, with all the complicated social functions such things entail. For others, competitive sports are a way to make a living. For yet others, competitive sports are the new opiate of the masses, functioning primarily to keep us from thinking about anything that matters. Take your pick; they all sound relatively true to me.

SPORT OR GAME OR BOTH?

Attempts are regularly made to distinguish between sports and games. Half a century ago, Roderick Haig-Brown, certainly one of the wisest and far-seeing writers on outdoor sport, emphasized the importance of the distinction. His mini-essay on the subject has an integrity, breadth, and skepticism that deserve quoting at length:

> All boys want to compete, and it is well that they should, but if they are to enjoy sport, as opposed to athletic contests, they must learn early to distinguish between the two. Sport is something enjoyed purely for its own sake, relaxing, healing and increasing; it is infinitely complex, limited in its scope only by the individual limitations of the man who pursues it; competition between men has no place in it and can only debase it. Athletic games and contests are

Canadian naturalist and angling writer Roderick Haig-Brown (1908–1976), one of the most respected philosopher figures of modern fly fishing, unequivocally opposed the competitive spirit in outdoor sport, saying that competition "has no place in it and can only debase it." ILLUSTRATION BY MARSHA KARLE FROM A 1965 PHOTOGRAPH BY MARY RANDLETT, OLYMPIA, WASHINGTON.

competition between men; easygoing sportsmanship once had a part in such affairs, sometimes still has; but for the most part it is lost in ruthless efficiency and something called the will to win. Sport is carried on generously within the limits of simple and largely unwritten rules developed to make it more interesting; the hunter or fisherman who does not stay within these rules kills his sport. Athletic contests are carried to the extreme limits of rules rigidly designed to prevent manslaughter and reduce cheating; the modern athlete who does not take every possible advantage of the rules is considered a deficient performer. There is room for both diversions in a boy's life or a man's life or a nation's life, but there should be no confusion between them.[1]

I've pointed out before that we tend to use the term "sport" quite casually, and very few of us adhere to any distinguishing language for making it clear whether we are talking about organized games or outdoor sports.[2] The lines are hardly clear, anyway. *Sports Afield* is almost all about hunting and fishing. *Sports Illustrated* is almost all about games.

I'm sure that some people would say that it is this loss of clarity of definition that is part of the modern problem; that it's in good part because modern recreationists, like some of Haig-Brown's "boys," were never taught the difference, so they now see no meaningful distinction between NASCAR and fly fishing. Merely that Haig-Brown thought all this involved only men and not women suggests how rapidly the social view of sport and games has changed since his time.

But I hope that the people who worry about that loss of clarity keep worrying about it and keep speaking out. The stakes are high here, and there is an important conversation to be had on how we wish to define fly fishing (if not NASCAR) in the future.

Though I will admit that I, too, am alternately appalled and saddened by some of what I see in modern fly fishing's drift into ever-flashier competitive events, that's not quite what this essay is about. I am concerned here with competition as an element of the past few centuries of the fly-fishing tradition.

I am concerned with this because in today's debates over the role of competitive events in the sport of fly fishing, history is being invoked to "prove" this or that on behalf of various viewpoints. History gets abused that way all the time, of course, in arguments over every imaginable subject. Most of us wouldn't know history if it came up and bit us on our breathables, but we love to think it's on our side.

So we might as well check and see what history has to say on the subject. Maybe it actually is on someone's side.

FLY FISHING AS A COMPETITIVE SPORT: WHEN AND HOW?

My longstanding interest in competitiveness among fly fishers was recently renewed by reading a defense of fly-fishing competitions in *Fly Fisherman*, in which the author said that, "Europeans have enjoyed fly-fishing competitions for centuries."[3] I gather from the context of remarks like this one that this long history of fly-fishing competition is seen as proof that fly-fishing competitions are okay today. After all, if our forefathers have been holding such competitions for centuries, surely today's competitions are nothing but an honorable part of a long tradition.

The critical reader may have already noticed a potential flaw in this attempt to invoke history to defend competitive fly-fishing events. Just because we've done something for hundreds of years doesn't necessarily mean it was okay then, much less now (think witch-burning or slavery). But let's let that flaw go for now and look at fly-fishing history specifically.

First, let's each recall our own experiences fishing with friends. Few of us could accurately claim that we have never felt a competitive moment when fishing with our pals. Competition plays a role in countless fishing tales in our literature, and though some of them are a bit unseemly, most fall within the realm of what we would still consider good sportsmanship. We had better start by admitting that we like to catch the most fish, and that often means outfishing someone else, and that it feels good to do that.

Three and a half centuries ago, no less ardent a gentlefisher than Izaak Walton himself endorsed this mild and very localized form of competition. While describing what made a good angler, he said, "... it is diligence, and observation, and practice, and an ambition to be the best in the art, that must do it. I will tell you, scholar, I once heard one [such angler] say, 'I envy not him that eats better meat than I do, nor him that is richer, or that wears better clothes than I do; I envy nobody but him, and him only, that catches more fish than I do.' And such a man is like to prove an angler; and this noble emulation I wish to you and all young anglers."[4]

What makes this comment by Walton especially interesting is that he is the authority that today's anti-competition commentators most often invoke to demonstrate that fly fishing's tradition has no room for such things as fly-fishing tournaments or one-fly contests, much less a fly-fishing world championship. That sort of thing, they say, is not in the "Waltonian" tradition.

And, though they may have missed this one finer point of Walton's view, they are still correct to invoke him that way. Even admitting that Walton was not much of a fly fisher, in his beautiful book he forever expressed much of the still-prevailing sentiment of angling as a gentle and nonbelligerent enterprise. As he did so, he wisely acknowledged that anglers do like to outfish each other.

We don't dare lean too hard on the 350-year-old pronouncements of a man who died long before the appearance of a society that could create and then support professional athletics on a multibillion-dollar scale. He was certainly speaking to us in his book, but let's be careful to read him in his own context. Whether

The writings of Izaak Walton (1593–1683), widely regarded as the philosophical father figure of British and American sport fishing, have almost nothing to say for or against the competitive spirit in angling. But because of the spiritual and contemplative tone of his *The Compleat Angler* (1653), Walton is often invoked by critics of the modern fly-fishing tournament.

ILLUSTRATION BY MARSHA KARLE, FROM AN ENGRAVING COURTESY OF THE AMERICAN MUSEUM OF FLY FISHING, MANCHESTER, VERMONT.

Walton's mild advocacy of some good-natured rivalry among anglers justifies NASCAR-on-the-South-Platte is another matter, and no doubt each of us will draw his or her own conclusions.

But if you are among those seeking Waltonian support for professional competitive fly fishing, you may read all the rest of Walton's writings without finding anything else to help you, and you will find much to suggest that you are off track. For Walton, angling was about quiet, and solitude, and gentleness, and beauty. If you could make that combination work with a little competitive edge added, more power to you. But it strains the historical record to get more than that from him, just as it strains the historical record to say with absolute certainty that Walton wouldn't love a day zooming around in a good bass boat. We just don't know.

This is not to suggest that competition, or competitiveness, seemed to be much on the minds of Walton's contemporaries, or on the minds of most of the angling writers between his time and the early 1800s. I have found no historical evidence of formal angling competitions—that is, organized competitions as opposed to a couple guys making a casual streamside wager between themselves—until the 1800s. And even then it looks like fly fishing was about the last type of sport fishing to join the contest.

I hope that in previous chapters I have made it clear that nineteenth-century anglers were at least as diverse in their personalities and passions as we are today. The most hard-core overachievers—William Stewart and David Webster come straight to mind—were not only driven to outfish the rest of the world, they were just as driven to outcompete their fellow fishing theorists. (Stewart: "If the sport of angling lies in the capture of fish, it seems evident that the more fish the better sport."[5])

There was not only competition in catching fish; there was competition between experts over whose special tactics were the best at catching fish—which was to say, whose book, flies, or other proprietary tackle were most worth buying; commerce was just another kind of competition.

Whether or not they engaged in formal fishing competitions, these Stewart-type anglers were by nature and personality ferociously intense about it all. The great increase in fishing-book production in the nineteenth century exposes more of the quirks and styles of that century's anglers, but I imagine that similarly disparate types fished the rivers of England in every previous century as long as fish hooks were known.

This reality—that there have always been personality types inclined to aggressive interaction with other fishermen—may be a sort of left-handed concession to those who want to believe that modern fly-fishing competitions are a natural outgrowth of the sport's traditions. But it's a fairly feeble concession. Just because human nature includes certain traits in its options doesn't prove those traits must necessarily be accommodated or celebrated in a given activity. If even Father Izaak endorsed a little friendly rivalry, who could doubt its presence anyway? Among the many personality types on the stream on any given day—out there with the overachievers, the underachievers, the hustlers, the jocks, the fashion-plates, the navel-gazers, the club-joiners, and all the rest of us who are usually several of these things at once—will surely be some William Stewarts, out to destroy the competition.

Today's professional fly-fishing competitions are a lot more flashy and commerce-driven than were Walton and his buddies, vying to catch the most dace and maybe making the loser buy the first round of ale that evening. But the difference between then and now is relative rather than absolute. The size of the audience, the formality of the rules, and the payoff of winning are much greater now, but the pro-competition crowd might well ask, "So what? If all we're doing is haggling over price here, why bother? What's the difference?" Interesting question.

IT ALL STARTED

So we're a diverse crowd and some of us are competitive by nature. No questioning those things. The historical existence of formal competitions among fly fishers is a different question entirely.

The British sporting historian Charles Chenevix Trench has described the rise of match fishing in the UK this way:

It all started during the nineteenth century in the English industrial north and midlands, where there were thousands of keen working-class anglers to whom trout-fishing was inaccessible owing to cost and distance. (In contrast, Scottish, Welsh, and Irish artisans had trout-fishing almost on the doorstep, so match-fishing has never been popular in the Celtic fringe.) Most of the rivers and canals they fished were polluted by their factories, so the fishing was not very good. Competition gave it just that excitement which can hardly be found solely in angling for small roach. At first competitions were local, on a pub or small club basis, enlivened by sweepstakes, winner take all. Inevitably, a National Federation of Anglers was formed in 1903; and in 1906 the first N.F.A. Annual Championship was held.[6]

None of this was about fly fishing, though we ought to recognize that fly fishing has inspired its own kind of competition. Casting competitions were held in the U.S. as early as 1860.[7] In fact, because of the evolving tackle available at the time, this is when competitions would first have become meaningful, which further suggests that even fly fishers needed only the right tackle and opportunities to very quickly find ways to formalize at least some aspects of the sport into competitive events.

The right tackle appeared by the mid-1800s or so. With the popularization of reels, silk lines, and modern metal guides on rods, fly casters were no longer restricted to the length of line that could be attached to the end of the rod. John Betts's researches have traced the development of false-casting and line-shooting, as nineteenth-century anglers availed themselves of the new and much more versatile equipment.[8] This equipment was essential to

At the inaugural tournament of the San Francisco Fly-Casting Club in Golden Gate Park, a replica of Izaak Walton's famous "fishing house" sat near the casting platform as a symbolic reminder of American angling's connection with the British tradition—and of the subtle and complicated connection between the Waltonian angling tradition and the formalized casting and angling competitions of more recent times.
FROM THE *AMERICAN FIELD*, MAY 19, 1894.

competition. Until a reel held abundant extra line for shooting, until a line could be shot (which is to say, until silk lines replaced knotted horse-hair lines), and until a rod could allow the line to pass smoothly through its guides while being shot, distance casting as we know it today was not possible. Distance casting was an essential ingredient in the mix needed to generate an interest in competitive casting, which has flourished ever since. Distance casting—and accuracy casting at distances beyond a couple rod lengths—constituted virtually all of the important components of competitive fly casting as it arose in the later 1800s.

But let's also keep in mind that competitive fly casting wasn't a fishing contest. Fly-casting contests are to fly fishing as rodeo is to ranching. Casting contests were independent of the streams and lakes where fishing took place. The contestants, some of whom were among the best-known fly fishers of the late 1800s in both England and America, were exercising a specific set of skills with, to use Haig-Brown's words, "extreme limits of rules" that controlled the entire process. Casting contests, to further follow Haig-Brown's terminology, took an element of the *sport* of fly fishing and turned it into a *game*.

Meanwhile, it was back on the real streams and lakes where competition, even in the nineteenth century, came up against the resistance and disapproval of people who saw fishing as being about something less adversarial. I have the impression that in the matter of competitiveness among anglers, nineteenth-century fishing writers tended to divide themselves into the two general categories that we still assign to them today. The instructional ("Practical," to use Stewart's term) writers were more likely to be all for the rapid harvest of fish and outfishing the other guy. The experiential (the storytellers) tended to take a less aggressive and demanding stance toward the fish, the river, their fellow anglers, and themselves.[9]

Stewart will serve as the type specimen of the former group. He was thought of as fanatical; if the word "obsessive" had been available, his contemporaries would have used it to describe him. One angler who knew him remarked that "a day out with Stewart was 24 hours of creeping and crawling."[10]

No one exemplified the second group better than Stewart's fellow Scot, the poet-scholar-angler Andrew Lang, whose 1891 book, *Angling Sketches*, remains one of the most charming of the era's fishing memoirs. Lang was a proto–Nick Lyons, self-deprecating,

humorous, and wise. His protestations of his own unworthiness as
an angler, whether real or just a pleasant literary stance, placed him
firmly in the camp of those of us who are simultaneously suspicious
and perhaps a little jealous of the masterful fish-catchers of our generation.

Lang did not feel a need to be expert at catching fish to perceive problems with competitive fishing. As a first-hand witness,
he lamented the rise of the late-nineteenth-century match-fishing
chronicled by Trench:

> That men should competitively angle shows, indeed, a
> great want of true angling sentiment. To fish in a crowd is
> odious, to work hard for prizes of flasks and creels and
> fly-books is to mistake the true meaning of the pastime.
> However, in this crowded age men are so constituted that
> they like to turn a contemplative exercise into a kind of
> Bank Holiday. There is no use in arguing with such
> persons.[11]

Notice that there is more than one complaint here. The
match-fisher lacked "true angling sentiment." Fishing lost much
of its Waltonian charm (Lang would have been intimately familiar
with Walton's book) when practiced in big crowds. Competition
was no substitute for contemplation. The competitive anglers,
crowding this or that water, ruined the fishing for the more contemplative types as well as for themselves.

There is also a whiff of class distinction here. The anglers,
including presumably Lang, who could afford some privacy were
better able to enjoy the luxuries of contemplative angling, while
the working-class crowd had to take what they could get, which

usually meant very small fish in the least desirable waters. Anglers who had enjoyed fishing relatively quiet public waters for many years were no doubt horrified by the abrupt appearance of the great heaving masses, turned out of a Sunday for a good fishing match. NASCAR couldn't be far behind.

THE VARIETIES OF THE COMPETITIVE IMPULSE

There is another intriguing byway in our consideration of the competitive, or at least score-keeping, aspects of sport fishing. As Tony Hayter's fascinating biography of Frederic Halford reveals, by the late 1800s and the rise of what we might still call the "scientific" school of anglers (they certainly saw themselves as such) symbolized by Halford and his dry-fly associates, a documentary rigor was an integral part of the sport. Halford's crowd often kept precise journals that remind me of Arnold Gingrich, who, sixty years later, would include an essay, "Trout by the Score," in his book, *The Well-Tempered Angler*. Scorekeeping has rarely been more subtly competitive than in these notes, in which the anglers were happily keeping track of their quest for success; the competition was, of course, still against one another, but it was just as much against the trout, the stream, and their previous catches. They were competing not only among themselves but each with himself. Leave it to fly fishing's greatest quantifiers to find so many ways to refine and enjoy their inherent competitive spirit.

But for the most part the complaints that have been expressed about competition in sport fall into two main categories. There are the objections to the formalizing of competition—the making of the sport into a game. And there are the objections to unbridled competitive urges among anglers who are not formally competing.

Lang's criticism of the former group will serve as an example of the type. The great American fly-fishing writer Theodore Gordon provided us with an equally heartfelt criticism of the latter group, in an article about Catskill fishing published in *Forest and Stream*, June 1908:

> There were many fishermen this year. Some men sit in a barroom all day, after engaging a couple of local anglers to fish for them. Their ideas of what constitutes sport are peculiar, but they usually return with a large number of trout. Doubtless they enjoy a fine reputation at home. Greed and the spirit of competition should have no place on the trout stream. It is amusing, however, to see a number of men trying to get ahead of each other and to fish all the best water first. We are not here to run foot races or to get the best of the other fellow. Take it easy, fish slowly and very probably you will have as much success as anyone.[12]

Here, Gordon falls well within the Waltonian camp. The pressure to catch fish, and to demonstrate one's prowess as a fisherman, leads to self-deception. The competitive urge not only takes the fun out of sport and causes general anxiety and an adversarial atmosphere on the stream, but probably adds nothing to your success. Might as well take it easy. As Walton's Ecclesiastical quote so famously put it, study to be quiet.

SO MUCH FOR HISTORY

I doubt that anyone who has invoked fly fishing's long literary and ethical tradition in support of today's high-visibility commercial fly-fishing competitions knows much about that tradition. In the first 400 or so years of the written record, let's say up until the middle of the twentieth century, the sport's most revered philosopher-thinkers—as distinguished from the sport's most admired technicians—without exception counseled a low-key approach to competition, if they approved of it at all. Among these folks, from Walton to Haig-Brown, the ideal angler was the one who did all he could to ensure that others had a chance at the best spot, and in other selfless ways sacrificed personal opportunities to give the advantage to fellow anglers.

Are these long-dead graybeards the people we should listen to today? They weren't lawmakers, you know; they were just advisors. Every generation of anglers before us had its share of people who pretty much ignored the day's philosophers and went for the competitive approach. Who is to say that the philosophers were right anyway?

We each get to make that judgment call. But whatever we decide, let's not fool ourselves into thinking we have some simple, monolithic History on our side. And let's remember that the people who have most favored competitiveness in fly fishing tended to be the guys who won most of the competitions, rather than the guys who took a larger, longer view of what fly fishing might mean in our lives.

For many years now, I've fished with Bud Lilly. Fishing with Bud is special because, thanks to his quiet generosity, you often get home from a day of "fishing with Bud Lilly" before you realize that you were the only one who fished much. Bud hardly made a cast. The casts he made may have been memorable and surely were more effective than yours, but at the time you probably didn't even notice how few of them there were.

Bud epitomizes that Waltonian tradition—and the once-a-guide-always-a-guide ideal—by enjoying a day's fishing in good part through the shared rewards of his fellow anglers' successes. And while few of us would argue that this is, indeed, a high and rarified form of fly fishing, just as few of us would be able to pull it off. We might rationalize our failure by saying, "Well, sure, if I spent as much time on the river as Bud Lilly does, I could afford to be that generous too." But in our hearts we know that if we can't "afford" it, we're choosing to live a smaller life and participate in a smaller sport, and that everybody should be that generous.

The Waltons, Haig-Browns, and Lillys may have raised the bar impossibly high for most of us, but we can at least appreciate the ideal that they've established. If we're going to compete at something, maybe we should compete at being uncompetitive.

TAKING IT PERSONALLY

History can only carry us so far in this kind of rumination. There are too many localized and highly specific little twists and turns in the inquiry. So I must take you out on the river now, and work my way through one of my own experiences with competitive fly fishing.

I'm going to do this by quoting from a letter I wrote to a fishing friend based on my notes after participating in the Jackson Hole One-Fly. I use the device of a letter because of its informality and because of its immediate specificity to the unique events that occur on any day astream.

I can tell you right off that I'm not going to try to trash this competition. The One-Fly is a justifiably honored and respected competition whose leaders have done a lot of soul-searching about what they're up to. The event has raised large amounts of money to support good conservation causes in the Jackson Hole area at the same time that it has allowed many, many fly fishers to have a great time fishing a lot of beautiful water for a lot of beautiful fish. I was pleased, even delighted, to participate, and I was excited to watch some terrifically skilled fishermen in action. I was impressed by the underlying commitment to fairness exhibited by the organizers, and I was grateful for the opportunity to exercise my own personal biases and skepticisms on a thoughtfully run competition. I doubt that I could have found one that would challenge my thinking more, or better clarify the ambivalence many of us feel about competitions.

I was invited to participate in the One-Fly as a member of the Grand Teton National Park Foundation team. The foundation is a nonprofit organization that raises money for the care of Grand Teton National Park, a cause dear to my heart. My friends at that park knew I loved to fish; they probably thought I was better at it than I was, but it was very nice of them to involve me.

Knowing I was going to participate, my friend asked me to let him know what I thought of the whole experience. My letter (slightly tidied up here for publication) was as much an attempt to explain it to myself as to him.

Dear Bob:

I see that lately *Fly Fisherman* has been running a dialogue in its opinion and letters departments among people who feel one way or the other about these competitive events, and judging from the growth in the events, I guess they're going to be with us at least for a while, so I don't think there's any hope of making them go away even if we were to decide that they are definitely all bad. So far I haven't felt any strong urge to enter that debate, though I do see some pretty feeble thinking on the part of the pro-event types, who are very full of self-justification and (surprisingly enough) even try to invoke history to back them up.

Though there was a lot of cheerful protestation among the people I talked to, who all maintained that this really was just for fun, it was pretty obvious that even those who said that most loudly had a competitive streak and didn't want to lose. It's very hard not to care about how you do, and the competitions, whatever else they may or may not do, can't help setting you up to respond competitively when you're put in that position. So that was there, and it was really plain.

This is very largely a crowd of comfortably well-off guys (and a number of women) who are accustomed to competition in their work lives, and who are probably also in most cases big fans of professional sports. If you take fly fishing and attach to it a modestly scaled-down version of the spectacle-enhancing attributes of NASCAR or the NFL (we were all issued matching shirts with logos, really high-grade stuff), you're going to set up the same spectacle-oriented mood. If you keep score, you're going to trigger some of those same conditioned responses in us that a tight NFL game does. So sure, you can stand back from all this staging and posturing and say, "Well, it's all in good fun," and that's going to be more or less true, but you've generated something outside the traditional approach that a few dozen generations of anglers had to fly fishing, and that's where people will disagree over what's "good."

Perhaps the biggest surprise, as far as things to think about, had only indirectly to do with the competitiveness. It had to do with how the competitiveness plays out in a catch-and-release fishery. Of course like most of these events, catch-and-release may greatly mitigate the potential for resource harm, though the people with a moral objection to catch-and-release would just see competition as yet another layer of outrage added to our cruel treatment of the fish ("You keep *score* of your torturing rate?!"). But what I saw on the second day of fishing, though it wasn't all that different from what I would see on any guided trip, really struck me as indicative of something troubling.

I have to explain the situation first. All the fishing was float fishing. Each boat had two anglers, each from a different team, and one guide. We traded off the front and back of the boat, and the guide divided his time between us when we stopped to wade. The guides were really great, as has practically every guide I've ever had been. They were having fun, though I am sure they were feeling the competition too.

Anyway, as soon as we stopped to wade fish, I noticed how thoroughly our guide had been scouting the river the previous days. He would march one or the other of us to a spot, not a stretch of water but a spot. He would say stand there, cast right up past that snag, about six inches out. There's a seventeen-and-a-half-incher there. We wouldn't always catch the fish, usually didn't, but when catch-and-release produces this level of familiarity with a stream, something rings hollow in the term "wild trout."

The trout aren't domesticated or tame, but they're getting a little too familiar for me to want to be fishing for them.

This is just a reality of catch-and-release fishing, anyway. If you fish a stream very often, you can actually get to know the fish as individuals. You're no longer fishing to see what the water has, you're fishing to take a fish, a certain fish, you know is there. I know that in many waters I fish, I'm fishing for fish that were caught the day before. But they're strangers to me, and I can, so far, live with that familiarity. It's the modern world, and I do have places I can escape it and have a chance of catching a fish that has never been caught before. So it doesn't seem out of control most of the time.

In the little freestone streams where I do most of my fishing, this hasn't happened to me. I haven't made that kind of effort to census the local fish, and I am still fishing spots that I know are generally likely to hold fish. I'm not sure I'm interested in fishing for a fish I know I've caught three times before, named Orville, who resides just under that bush, and who demands a 5X tippet. That's too tame a *situation*, whether the *trout* is wild or not.

So. Add that revelation to the uneasiness of knowing that the guide and I are there to produce inches of fish, and we're essentially trying to high-grade the fishable population for those fish that will serve us best in the contest. It made for an intellectual restlessness about the whole enterprise that I didn't enjoy feeling.

When a sport is changing, or even when a sport appears to be changing and its practitioners disagree over the realness and magnitude of the change, restlessness is vitally important. It keeps us thinking and watching, keeps us questioning ourselves.

We can and will each convince ourselves that our own approach to this is the best one. If we are open-minded enough, we will convince ourselves that it is the best one *for us*. Ted Leeson summed this up beautifully in *The Habit of Rivers* (1994):

> It is curious to see how each fisherman will fix the limits of his own sport. Some use only the dry fly; others fish only to the rise, still others cast only feather-light rods or tiny patterns. No two anglers I've ever fished with defined their boundaries in quite the same way or devised quite the same rationale for what they did. We each map the borders of a world and fish in an envelope of our own making that is both intensely personal and flagrantly arbitrary. If pressed, we can give "reasons" for where we drew the lines, though often enough these are equally capricious and persuasive only to the likeminded.[13]

We do this all the time. We like or dislike strike indicators, weighted flies, weighted lines, bamboo rods, and countless other elements of theory, tactic, and ethic, and we construct personally convincing narratives of how we want to go fishing. Too much of the time the narratives attempt not only to be "reasons" but also proof of the superiority of our specific take on the whole sport.

If nothing else convinces us that we are deeply competitive, our need to justify ourselves this way should. If we become Waltonian anglers only to prove that we're above the fray and somehow superior to our fellow anglers—to feel good about ourselves rather than to do good because it's the right thing—then we're betraying the sport as surely as we could in any other way.

WHAT I CAN'T KNOW, AND WHAT I HAVE TO DO WITH IT

I can't know what Walton, Gordon, or Haig-Brown would make of the very concept of a "world champion" of fly fishing, but I suspect they'd find it a little odd. On the other hand, lots of people apparently just love the whole competitive scene, and as long as they stay out of my way, I'm not sure how much right I have to object. After all, maybe I'm missing something in the competitions—something besides the pretty shirts and gravy-train of cool tackle—that makes those people all seem so happy in the pictures. I need to remember that great question that one of Sterne's characters asked in *Tristram Shandy*, "And so long as a man rides his hobby-horse peaceably and quietly along the King's highway, and neither compels you or me to get up behind him,—pray, sir, what have either you or I to do with it?"[14]

That admitted, it isn't the uncomfortably self-congratulatory image of the competitions that interests me most anyway. What I'm curious about is what the Gordons and Haig-Browns seem to be expecting of me instead.

Here's the question. Is the traditional zero-tolerance for competition just another one of fly fishing's unattainable ideals? Most of us know we'll never cast like the Rajeffs, or tie flies like the Harrops, or do much of anything else like the real experts. Is it the same with these questions of sportsmanship? Assuming the Waltons and Haig-Browns were right, how seriously should we expect to live up to their high standards? How often did *they* live up to them?

While admitting that it wouldn't hurt any of us to be a little nicer on the stream, I'm also prepared to confess that I'm probably not ready for the leap to full noncompetitive saintliness. I really like it when I outfish my big brother; he has a gift for original excuses that I would miss if we abandoned our mild and entirely jovial competition.

Besides, as an almost-altruistic angler I have the written permission of fly fishing's historical heavyweights not to care too much when my brother happens to outfish *me*. Unlike the world championship, altruism pays both ways, whether you're the winner or the loser.

And that, I would insist, sounds like a pretty good code to live by.

CHAPTER FIVE

IF THE FISHES WILL BE PATIENT

Fly Fishing, Wild Rivers, and the Legions of the Dammed

ONE DAY HENRY DAVID THOREAU SAT IN A CANOE ON A Massachusetts river, looking at a dam that cut off and destroyed a famous shad run. In his thoughts that day, he found a wistful solace in the long view:

> Perchance, after a few thousands of years, if the fishes will be patient, and pass their summers elsewhere meanwhile, nature will have leveled the Billerica dam, and the Lowell factories, and the Grass-ground River run clear again, to be explored by new migratory shoals. . . .[1]

Thoreau, eyewitness to these grimier truths of the Industrial Revolution, knew that the wait would be a long one. But perhaps even he couldn't have envisioned the phenomenal reach of the dam-building impulse in the world's rivers.

Anglers, like most people who believe in conservation, often have a hard time loving dams, whether the small ones that only plug up some obscure neighborhood drainage or the spectacular architectural monuments that transform the landscape, economics, and culture of entire regions. But our relationship with these vexing structures has never been simple.

Nor is it new. In fact, by the time that British anglers began to publish books about fishing, they and their European relatives were already long engaged in a world of artificial reservoirs created behind countless small dams. The dam was a fact of life for the angler. Among others, Leonard Mascall's *A Booke of Fishing with Hooke & Line* (1599), Gervase Markham's *The Pleasures of Princes* (1611), Thomas Barker's *The Art of Angling* (1651), Izaak Walton's *Compleat Angler* (1653), and James Chetham's *The Angler's Vade Mecum* (1681) all contained, either in their original edition or in subsequent editions, substantial advice on the management of fish ponds. Some even instructed you how to build them and provided ample advice on all you'd need to know about many practical matters—the best slope for the pond's bottom, which fish species will thrive under which circumstances, which fish species should not be mixed, practical natural history of pond life, and how to keep a pond healthy and productive for many years.

These anglers were perfectly comfortable with the fundamental idea of impounding water and with the creation of artificial fisheries, either for sporting use or for simple meat production. Perhaps dams aren't quite in our genes, but they're certainly in our culture, which is probably more important.

Since the Middle Ages anglers have happily explored the fishing opportunities of a broad array of reservoirs, mill ponds, and other partly or wholly artificial waters—most of which were originally created for other utilitarian purposes and then adopted by fish and the fishermen who pursued them. FROM *FRANK FORESTER'S FISH AND FISHING OF THE UNITED STATES AND BRITISH PROVINCES OF NORTH AMERICA* (1849).

I suppose I'm typical of many fly fishers, especially those with roots in the flatlands, in having fished in more small impoundments—farm pond, county reservoir, leveed swampland—than I could ever list. The first place I ever cast a fly was a small man-made lake—part of a system of local levees in the farm country thereabouts—in central Ohio (this site had added cultural relevance as a skinny-dipping destination). It wasn't until I started writing this that I remembered that this pretty little lake had the desperately uninspired name of "Dam Four."

And I'm probably also typical of many anglers who have traveled considerable distances to fish in some dam-altered drainage (Maine's Grand Lake Stream comes to mind first for me) whose engineered waters are now genuinely historic fishing meccas. We savor and celebrate countless memories of these angling opportu-

The Atlantic salmon is only the most glamorous and well-publicized of several anadromous fish species whose numbers have been catastrophically reduced by the construction of dams. This fine engraving, celebrating both the fish and the rivers it inhabits, appeared in T. C. Hofland, *The British Angler's Manual* (1839). COURTESY OF THE AMERICAN MUSEUM OF FLY FISHING, MANCHESTER, VERMONT.

nities, and we owe all those memories to dams. Dams are deep in our *angling* culture too.

Besides, American society has always felt an urgent need for dams. Maybe we didn't like what Lowell, Massachusetts, and a hundred other industrial centers turned into, but the nation had work to do, right? And how many people in Thoreau's day would ever have imagined that we'd end up with dams on all but one of the country's major rivers—and smaller dams by the thousand on the lesser streams?

But we always knew they were a mixed blessing. That day in his canoe, Thoreau recalled that even as the dam he pondered was under construction, some doubtful souls insisted that it was not

worth the losses of fish that would result. Fish were just less important than were all the things that dams gave society. For fly fishers,
the near-total loss of Atlantic salmon from their historic range in
New England has been the most famous casualty of the dams, but
their effects have long been national in scope, reaching into every
major drainage in the United States.

MONSTERS

And yet, aside from the harm they've done, dams have often played
a role in shaping American fly fishing. Among the most famous
native trout in American History—for both biological and sporting reasons—were the brook trout of the Rangeley Lakes of
Maine. Long known to and caught by local Native Americans,
these grand fish came to national prominence in the mid-1800s.
But fame came slowly, partly because of their remote home waters,
partly because some of the anglers who knew about them were
reluctant to spread the word, and partly because when the word
did get out it was a pretty difficult word to believe.

One of the early white settlers in the Rangeley region, Joshua
Rich, recalled fishing Mooselookmeguntic Lake when there was
little or no development, even before the dams. Looking back
from his old age in the 1880s, he recalled a fishing trip in 1854
with a combination of regret at the waste he participated in and a
lingering amazement at the fish.

This was truly "fishing"—not "angling." It was accomplished
at night, with a torch to attract the fish to the boat and a spear to
catch them:

> I remember one night at Trout Cove when an old hunter
> by the name of Leaverett and myself took in one night

one hundred beauties which weighed the next morning six hundred pounds. Those we sold to old Pearly Smith, the trap maker, at four cents a pound salted, and took our pay in steel beaver traps.

The most successful bait was grasshoppers in August and first of September, and spawn later. In the spring fishing, fresh squirrel meat was as good as anything I ever used.

We had never heard of pot-fishers or poachers, and there had been no law enacted against the taking of trout any way we chose, and we went at it the quickest possible way.[2]

If those one hundred fish *averaged* six pounds, we can only daydream about what the big ones must have weighed. Rangeley brook trout in excess of ten pounds were reliably reported, while fish between twelve and seventeen pounds were much less reliably, but intriguingly, reported.[3]

The eventual popularization and consequent diminution of the fabulous brook-trout fishery of the Rangeleys has been chronicled in several books, including Herbert Shirrefs's *The Richardson Lakes: Jewels in the Rangeley Region* (1995), and Nick Karas's *Brook Trout* (1997). In the 1850s and early 1860s, a few parties of sportsmen from distant cities made their way to the area, and the word began to spread. In 1863, fly fisher George Shepard Page returned from the Rangeleys to New York City with eight trout that averaged six and a half pounds. The largest weighed eight and three quarters pounds.

With considerable fanfare, Page presented the fish to prominent citizens, and word of the gift reached the local papers. Published reports of these tremendous trout were followed by an outcry of skepticism from local sportsmen. Page had anticipated this reaction, and one of the nation's foremost fish authorities was engaged to settle the matter of what species these fish were:

> Then there broke out an excitement among anglers altogether without precedent. Scores of letters were sent to the papers which had presumed to call these brook trout—some of them interrogative, others denunciatory, others theoretical, and others flatly contradictory. The Adirondacks had never yielded a brook-trout which weighed more than 5 lbs., and that, therefore, must be the standard of brook-trout the world over. But Mr. Page had foreseen the violent skepticism which was sure to manifest itself, and had sent a seven-pounder to Professor Agassiz, who speedily replied that these monster trout were genuine specimens of the speckled or brook trout family, and that they were only found in large numbers in the lakes and streams at the head waters of the Androscoggin River, in North-western Maine.[4]

In the Rangeleys, the first dams had arrived before the sport fishermen. Conveniently, dams built originally to facilitate the movement of logs or provide power for local sawmills required much of the same infrastructure—roads, lodging, stores—that fishing camps and resorts did. Thus, the dams did tend to concentrate the fishermen. Upper Dam, probably the most famous Rangeley dam in terms of its role in American fly-fishing lore, was first constructed some time between 1845 and 1853, though it was later moved and enlarged.[5]

Anglers were quick to realize that the region's relatively few strategically placed dams could offer good fishing in the pools and runs downstream. An angler visiting in 1872 left this account of the pool at Upper Dam:

> There is a glorious pool at the foot of the dam. In this pool big trout were swimming, for we actually saw them, and breaking water with a nonchalance and a tantalizing sense of security which was positively maddening. Around this pool, which was about 80 feet in diameter, were seven, I do not exaggerate, ardent anglers, armed with huge bamboo poles, some twenty feet in length and three inches at the butt. They were fishing with minnows, worms, spawn, in fact every lure that was illegitimate and unscientific, and in lathe constructed cars, which were tethered near the pool, we saw dozens of magnificent trout, weighing from four to seven pounds.
>
> Getting up early, we were able to fish from good locations and caught five trout weighing 27½ pounds, the largest being 8½ pounds.[6]

So there is no question that fishing the dam pool was exciting and, at least before overfishing diminished the trout population, full of promise.

Nor is there any doubt that dams played a central role in immortalizing some great moments in American angling history in the Rangeleys. On July 1, 1924, Carrie Stevens, whose husband was a local guide, cast her newly created streamer, the Gray Ghost, into the Upper Dam Pool and caught an award-winning six-pound, thirteen-ounce brook trout that launched her career as one of Maine's most original fly tiers. For all the excitement caused by the earlier stories of great fishing, Stevens's big fish, caught on her

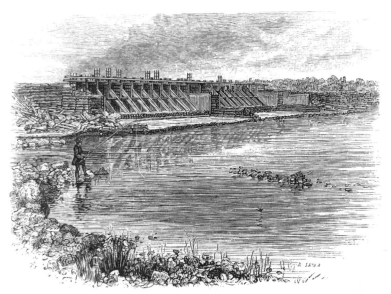

Upper Dam, between Upper Richardson Lake and Mooselookmeguntic Lake in Maine's famous Rangeley Lakes Region, has been a famous fly-fishing destination for nearly a century and a half. FROM ALBERT MAYER, EDITOR, *SPORT WITH GUN AND ROD* (1883).

very famous fly, has probably done the most to keep Upper Dam Pool in the memory of modern fly fishers.[7]

But most of the time, for all the fanfare given these and other episodes of fishing at the Rangeley dams, the dams themselves seem not to have been all that important a part of the greater Rangeley fishing experience. As Rich's account and other early reports make clear, the Rangeleys didn't need dams to produce incredible fish. All the dams did was provide the less mobile fishermen with a few very handy spots where the fishing seemed to be very good much of the time.

Seymour's lengthy 1877 *Scribner's* article, like others of the time, made it clear that almost all of the serious fishing for really big trout was done by anglers scattered throughout the region.

Guides were highly recommended, to help the visiting angler find the good spots in all that undifferentiated water.[8] The dams didn't support the only good fishing, nor were they even necessary to attract fishermen. Indeed, according to Seymour, in the 1870s, the mile and a half of water downstream from Upper Dam was "so steadily and thoroughly fished" that the fishing club on that water "lately secured the passage of a law by the Maine Legislature prohibiting any fishing there for a term of five years." While Seymour anticipated fast action in that stretch of water when fishing again resumed, the Rangeleys apparently had plenty of other great fishing waters for anglers to enjoy while the Upper Dam water was closed.

What the enthusiastic accounts of angling on the Rangeleys seem to lack entirely is any meaningful comments on the dams themselves. If these anglers found the dams unfortunate or inconvenient in any way, they did not have much to say about it, at least in the articles and books I've read from that place and time. The dams, as dams, didn't seem to matter to them.

This shouldn't be surprising. Later-arriving anglers, by which I mean most of those who found their way to the Rangeleys following Page's revelation of the big brook trout, would probably have seen the dams as little more than part of the scenery. For most fishermen, the dams were the long-established status quo, rather than something to necessarily care about one way or another—they were just dams. Dams were appearing everywhere in America at the time, and though, as Thoreau had shown, some people disapproved of this one or that, few people spoke out against the general "progress" they represented.

And what Rangeley angler would object? When you could go to Maine, stand by what must have seemed to most people like a huge dam (Upper Dam was 1,500 feet long), and see enormous trout swirling around within easy casting distance, you would have to have been utterly daft to complain.

In other parts of the country, dams would eventually become a much more important part of fly fishing, but in ways that no one in the Rangeleys would even have dreamed of.

INFANT FISHERIES

I bought my treasured copy of Jim Gasque's *Hunting and Fishing in the Great Smokies* (1948) used and lucked into one that was signed by the author ("Asheville, NC, Aug/48 *Jim Gasque*"). Published the year I was born, it is a guide to fishing and hunting in the region in and around Great Smoky Mountains National Park (there was and is no legal hunting in the park itself). It's a book from that wonderful era of outdoor writing when outdoorspeople, at least the ones whose pictures you could see and whose conversations you could read in magazines and books, looked and talked more or less like Mark Trail.

It's also from that wonderful era of Borzoi Books from Alfred Knopf, surely one of the pinnacles in the five-century history of sporting book publishing. Gasque was joined by Ray Bergman, Jack O'Connor, Russell Annabel, and Andy Russell in the phenomenal list of Borzoi authors. These were writers who, even if they weren't the greatest literary craftsmen, were unquestionably the greatest outdoor writers. And they were made greater by their association with each other and with the imprint they distinguished.

Maybe one reason I like books from those days is that they had a simpler idea of the world. Gasque's book has its harsher moments—including a genuine fist fight along a stream—but the mood of these books is more accurately captured by Gasque's color frontis, a painting of a splendidly dated, garishly colored fishing scene.

Untitled, this picture is nearly what the art historians would call a "primitive," with its own childlike sense of perspective and prettiness. In the left foreground, the tall, ruggedly-clad, strong-jawed angler stands in the shallows of a tree-lined stream, his fly rod bent with a good fish. In the middle distance—just to the right of the obligatory waterfall and perhaps looking down at the stream to where our angler's line disappears into the water—is a dark animal. At first, subconsciously applying my western wildlife–conditioned search image, I thought that this animal looked like a cross between a wolf and sheep. This seemed unusually cryptic imagery for the time. But after a minute I realized it was supposed to be a bear.[9]

From that idyllic opening scene, *Hunting and Fishing in the Great Smokies* is continuously a nice, happy book, made more so by its tales of bears and bear hunting, boars and boar hunting, and practical guidance on hunting smaller game. There's even a too-short chapter on the legendary Plott hounds so long popular among southern hunters, and an embarrassingly blatant plug for a local resort that had clearly treated, or was soon going to treat, Gasque very well.

But re-reading the book now, just sixty years after it was published, I am belatedly struck by what it lacks. Sure, it's almost devoid of postmodern cynicism, of entomology, of incessant expensive-tackle fetishism, and of numerous other modern angling-writing necessities and affectations. But it's missing something else, something that a similar book written today simply couldn't be without. It's missing the tailwaters.

Actually, it started to tell the tailwater story. Or, more accurately put, it told the start of the story, because the story had only just begun when the book was published.

Part one was about trout streams, with a few smallmouth streams thrown in. Gasque revealed himself as an enthusiastic fly fisher in the pragmatic Bergman mode—an enthusiasm he applied widely in the second part of the book, which was about lakes. Here, Gasque focused mostly on a few big reservoirs, most of them brand new hydroelectric or flood-control projects built by the Tennessee Valley Authority, near but not in Great Smoky Mountains National Park.

As I say, in 1948 these reservoirs were new. The ones he mentioned, including Fontana and Hiwassee, had only been finished in that decade. Gasque shared the excitement of discovery and exploration of these immense new fisheries. His enthusiasm was obvious. As far as he or anyone else knew or planned, the exciting fishing of the future around there was going to be in the lakes, with short forays up a few favorite feeder streams. Yes, there was really cold water rushing into each dam's tailrace, and perhaps a few people knew its potential, but it hadn't yet registered on the consciousness of many anglers.

Only twenty-three years later, Dave Whitlock, in one of the important early articles celebrating the tailwaters for a new generation of fly fishers, would look back on the rapid change that occurred in recreational fishing near the reservoirs since Gasque's time:

Perhaps a few farsighted biologists foresaw the advent of ideal environmental conditions for stocking trout, but this was certainly not the motive that inspired the projects in Tennessee as well as in other surrounding states. Later, it was noticed that these tail waters soon became almost void of native warm-water species as cold water was released from the hydroelectric facilities. This situation encouraged experiments and eventually rainbow and brown trout were introduced. But it has taken years to fully understand the new problems, to adopt practical stocking programs, to adjust laws and seasons and to use the fantastic potential of this infant fishery.

During the 40s, 50s and 60s practically every state south and west of the Mason-Dixon line has experienced dam building across many of its free-flowing streams and rivers. Many of these created suitable conditions for tail-water fisheries.[10]

Historian Kenneth Owens, who has written the most authoritative historical overview of how the tailwater fishery phenomenon has affected fly fishing, takes an even more absolute view than Dave did, saying that "prior to construction, no one—not fisheries biologists, and certainly not fly fishers—had an inkling of what impact bottom-release high dams would have on downstream fisheries, and certainly the planning stages for these USBR projects did not envision the creation of blue ribbon tailwaters."[11]

Tailwater trout streams, whether the dam upstream was built for flood control, irrigation, or hydroelectric power generation (and recognizing that those different functions result in different water-management strategies), are now a big deal. They have become many of the most exciting fly-fishing destinations in the United States. A list of just some of those phenomenally productive tailwater fisheries—the Bighorn, the Missouri, the San Juan, the South and North Plattes, the White, the Frying Pan, the West Branch of the Delaware, the Green—reads like a litany of trout-stream dreams. In the past half-century or so these wonderful new trout fisheries have attracted passionate and skilled constituencies, and have generated their own theories, methods, literature, and folklore.[12] At first glance, they seem to give the lie to the old saying among conservationists that "They aren't making trout streams any more."

But just like all those older, lower dams—the ones that, starting even before Thoreau's time, were killing off countless runs of salmon, shad, and other anadromous fish at the same time that they were contributing to the untold devastation wrought by the logging and other industrial development that they facilitated—the tailwaters would eventually be recognized as mixed blessings. Fly fishers didn't care much about the complications—remember our awed angler standing at Upper Dam Pool watching an eight-pound brookie swim toward his fly, and imagine his descendant similarly standing by the White River watching an eight-pound brown swim by. But that did not mean the complications didn't matter.

THE BEST WAY TO WIPE OUT FISH

In the twentieth century, as advancing dam technology enabled ambitious water managers to think really big, the effects on native fish and native aquatic ecosystems were both comprehensive and catastrophic. Huge dams across huge rivers upped the ante, as every secondary, tertiary, and progressively smaller drainage upstream felt the effects of each new dam.[13]

The Columbia River, a giant poster child among today's dam damners, provides the definitive example of this process in action.

The best short description of what happened to the Columbia River was given me by a fisheries biologist friend who worked on salmon management there. He put it this way: Imagine that one hundred years ago, Americans felt no need for the irrigation water or hydroelectric power that the Columbia could provide if dammed. But imagine that instead, Americans had a furious desire to eliminate the Columbia's incredible runs of salmon and steelhead—let's say they just couldn't stand the sight of the stinking things anymore. Well, those Americans could not have dreamed up a more comprehensive means of wiping out the fish than by building the more than 130 dams that they eventually built for other reasons.[14] It was recently estimated that almost all of 1,200-plus-mile length of the Columbia River mainstem is slackwater.

Dams, we have discovered, are about the most technologically effective anti-salmon/shad/steelhead weapon that humans have ever perfected. Unlike pollution, which can also devastate fish populations, dams keep working year after year. Pollution, as terrible as its effects are, requires you to keep pumping filth into the river if you want it to keep doing its worst.

By contrast, nice clean dams do the same job with little more than a few million cubic yards of cement. And at no extra charge, dams will also dramatically alter the temperature and chemistry of the whole aquatic ecosystem downstream, build immense silt deposits upstream, screw things up for all sorts of less glamorous native life forms in both directions, and otherwise pile insult and injury on the ecological system.[15]

Though the dam builders would have their way for a long time, even by the beginning of the twentieth century, public attitudes had begun to change. Dams have always been important in the American conservation movement, from its earliest days.[16] The growth of the modern conservation movement—especially that part of the movement as concerned with protecting wild places as with protecting the wildlife that depends upon those places for existence—from fledgling to mature can be symbolically bracketed between two milestone battles over dams: the Hetch Hetchy reservoir in Yosemite National Park, which was approved by Congress in 1913 after a bitter struggle with early conservationists, and the Echo Park Dam, which conservationists prevented from being built in the canyon wildernesses of Dinosaur National Monument in 1956.[17] The Echo Park controversy was, literally, a watershed event. More dams would be built after 1956, but the builders would always work under the shadow of Echo Park and the knowledge that they were no longer the only people with political muscle on the natural resource management scene.

In this sense, dams gave conservationists a way in, a focus for their concerns and ambitions. I'm not sure that should make us grateful to dams, but it is true that sometimes a problem has to be exposed in a really concentrated form before it can be fought. Dams concentrate many things, and attention is one of them.

In my neighborhood in Montana, this growing historic opposition to dams is best represented by a remarkable and heroic sustained effort by anglers and other local interest groups in stopping the U.S. Army Corps of Engineers from building the Allenspur Dam on the Yellowstone River, just south of Livingston. There but for the labors of the great fly-shop owner Dan Bailey and his friends, the beautiful area known as Paradise Valley would now be just another thirty-mile-long lake, drowning not just the river but some of the world's most famous spring creeks. On the Yellowstone, it all came down to the nation's last free-flowing major river before people finally said "enough."

SO?

So why talk about this here? What's the point of griping about dams again? Haven't we all heard this story, and seen it happen close to home?

Well, yes, we have, and most of us are tired of hearing about it. But there are intriguing developments brought on by the dam-building era, and they have some interesting effects on modern fly fishers.

One involves angling society. When promoters of dams used to proclaim the endless benefits of this or that proposal for a new one, they invariably mentioned recreation, and at least implied that the public would be thrilled with all the good fishing available in the new dam's reservoir. Sometimes this was even true. After all, replacing the narrow corridor of a free-flowing river with many thousands of acres of lake and many miles of shoreline must have seemed like a huge gain to the boating angler, and many reservoirs have become justly famous for their fishing. Even a serious fly fisher like Jim Gasque bought the TVA's pitch in 1948, pointing out that when the Hiwassee Dam went in, "for twenty-two miles the Hiwassee River has been changed from a fluctuating stream of little potential worth to a blue lake impounded behind a 1,287-foot dam."[18] To the public ear in Gasque's day, that sounded terrific. Today, at least to many public ears, it sounds less so. Many of us like the idea of hiking along, fishing, photographing, birding, or just looking at the winding river more than doing any of the same things by the lake.

For much of the history of American dam building, the marketing of dams as great recreational improvements on the landscape has largely eluded fly fishers. As much as many of us love stillwaters, and as spectacular as are some of the fly-caught fish from the large lakes, big-water reservoir fishing seems unlikely ever to match the modern fly fisher's passion for running water. Compare the number of lake-related destination articles (very few) in the fly-fishing magazines with the number of stream-related stories (almost all).

As Dave Whitlock said, fly fishers certainly were never a consideration in the thinking and planning of the TVA and other dam-building authorities. The tailwater fisheries so many of us now enjoy, as grand as they have become, were a tacked-on afterthought—a lucky fringe benefit of something that was originally done for other reasons, and for other fishermen.

I'm not sure what all the reasons are for this compartmentalization of fisher types, but I suspect that there are issues of social stratification at work here, and that even if we were more interested in the big reservoirs, we fly fishers just don't mix very well with the other crowds that dominate these places. I'll leave the sociological fine points for others to consider. The lesson may be that we fly fishers do have some political clout, but we're still the negligible small fry in the bigger picture of managing the nation's major rivers.

PALIMPSEST ANGLING

Tailwaters are ecological palimpsests—new river ideas written over the top of old river ideas. They are trout fisheries built upon the wreckage of whatever native aquatic ecosystem was there before the dam went in.

This brings us back to the often-repeated celebration of tailwaters, that they disprove the old saying that "they're not making trout streams anymore." Tailwaters don't create rivers—they replace rivers with different rivers. Before the 1960s, when Yellowtail Dam turned the Bighorn River in Montana into a phenomenal trout fishery, there already was a historic Bighorn River there, and just because its "sauger, catfish, burbot, goldeye and many Cyprinid species had never seen an angler's hook" doesn't convince everybody today that either the dam or the new fishery were necessarily a good thing.[19]

We each get to decide whether we should wallow in retroactive guilt as we make another cast on our favorite tailwater—after all, the dam wasn't built so we could do this—but we would be wise to keep in mind that this great new fishing comes at a price that some people even in our own ranks regard as too high. A few years ago, angler Chris Proctor expressed this ambivalence quite strongly in *Fly Fisherman* magazine. In an outburst still rare among fly fishers, Proctor criticized the tailwater fisheries of the West:

> No one wants to mention the fact that these tailwater trout fisheries should not exist—that collectively they are the product of shortsighted and short-term, environmentally destructive dam-building thinking, which we should have opposed with all of the same energy we now harness to oppose destructive damming of Atlantic-salmon spawning rivers, or destruction of good stream habitat anywhere.[20]

Proctor singled out as an example the Green River in Utah, which "should be inhabited by squawfish and other currently endangered species that need periodic floods and silt-laden water to thrive. Instead, it is a tailwater, inhabited by exotics imported from other drainages and other continents, and sustaining a very lucrative guide and drift-boat industry, which of course, has an interest in its own survival."[21]

To the mixed legacy of the tailwaters we might add another new development, and that's our continually changing understanding of what dams do and how their effects go on. A recent study of changes in the fish populations on the Ozarks' White River downstream from Beaver Dam (which became fully operational in 1965) revealed that the abrupt change in the river when it became a tailwater did not result in an equally abrupt, stable new community of fish species. Apparently, more than forty years later the aquatic community is still sorting itself out (and continues to lose its few remaining native species).[22] We don't yet know all we will eventually know about these systems.

UNDAMMING RIVERS

Setting aside for the moment the larger questions of the worth of our thoroughly dammed national watershed to society in general, it is hard to look at any hypothetical balance sheet and conclude anything except that these dams caused massively tragic harm to North America's luxurious richness and diversity of wild fisheries. You don't even have to go inland to establish this. The destruction or alteration of anadromous species' migratory patterns along both coasts is by itself an overwhelming tally against dams. Considering that throughout the dam-building era in this country the interests of fishermen were among the lowest considerations, it's probably surprising we're not worse off than we are. It is a testament to our adaptability and resourcefulness as sportsmen that we've found so many ways, some of them very good, to get along in the new fisheries world created by all these dams.

And though it's a faint change so far, there seems little doubt that, step by tiny step, we are entering a new era in the saga of the damming of American rivers. Here and there, there is actually serious work underway to remove this or that dam or even a series of dams, usually in the face of hostile, effective opposition from all the people who feel advantaged by the dam's services. But we may now be removing them faster than we're building them. Dozens of dams, usually small ones, are scheduled for removal each year, and though anglers can't claim credit for all of them (some of them are just too old to be safe), we are potential beneficiaries of the changes in the river systems, especially those with anadromous fish.

The removal of dams has itself become a very visible element of the conservation movement. To use one of society's odd new ways of measuring the significance of absolutely anything, run a Google search on "dam removal," and choose from more than 30,000 entries—about upcoming dam removal projects, about current fights over dam removals, and even about how to remove a dam yourself. In these many dialogues, rarely do the needs of fish and fishermen go unmentioned, and sometimes they get the most attention.

Some dams become symbols of the whole trend.[23] Of the ones removed so far, perhaps the 162-year-old Edwards Dam, on Maine's Kennebec River, has most caught the imagination of the conservation-minded public, because its removal in 1999 was accompanied by so much celebratory fanfare and because it was on a big river, one that drained about twenty percent of the state of Maine. At least nine migratory fish species, some quite rare and several of great potential economic value, now have a far better chance of surviving or even flourishing again.

For me, another dam stands for this hopeful movement toward unchoked aquatic ecosystems. The Elwha Dam, on Washington's Olympic Peninsula, was built in 1911 and blocked most of the Elwha River drainage. It is especially interesting to anglers; its

The Glines Canyon Project, one of the two aging hydroelectric dams soon to be removed from the Elwha River on Washington's Olympic Peninsula, is symbolic of the new era of dam removal, in which fisheries restoration issues have become significant in society's changing view of dams. The Glines Canyon dam, constructed in the 1920s, and the Elwha Dam (constructed between 1910 and 1913) a few miles downstream, have diminished or destroyed the runs of ten native anadromous fish species. Lake Mills, upper left, has trapped more than 13 million tons of sediment and dramatically altered the ecological setting in northern Olympic National Park. NATIONAL PARK SERVICE PHOTOGRAPH, OLYMPIC NATIONAL PARK.

removal is promoted heavily on the basis of fisheries restoration. Between them, the Elwha Dam and the Glines Canyon Dam, eight miles upstream, eliminated salmon and steelhead access to seventy miles of river and tributaries that a century ago were famous for outstanding fishing. Almost all of this water is in Olympic National Park, and the additional political and popular leverage provided by that special circumstance has long given dam-removal advocates cause for optimism. But even here, and even

Eleanor Chittenden with a large Elwha River steelhead in about 1907. Chittenden, the daughter of the famous western engineer and historian Hiram Chittenden, caught this fish shortly before the river was inundated behind two dams and the runs of anadromous fish such as this were eliminated. Removal of these dams may be imminent, allowing the runs to recover. ASAHEL CURTIS PHOTOGRAPH COURTESY OF THE WASHINGTON STATE HISTORICAL SOCIETY, TACOMA, WASHINGTON.

though in 1992 Congress authorized the Secretary of the Interior to remove the dams and restore the fisheries, removal still seems some way off in the future; the most recent predictions are for removal of the dams in 2009. I hope so, but I'm not going to hold my breath. There's progress, but it's mighty slow.

But I suppose that could be the motto of the whole dam-removal enterprise. Dam decommissioning isn't for the impatient; there's bureaucratic process and logistical complications galore, to say nothing of a lot of people who don't want the dams removed for reasons they firmly believe are right.[24]

There are an estimated 75,000 dams of at least six feet in height in the United States. Five thousand of those are at least forty-five feet high.[25] The removal of a few symbolically significant dams isn't likely to change the world of fly fishing. But it surely will change the world for those fly fishers in the neighborhood of the dismantled dams, as well as for those of us who are enchanted by the ecological wonder and fascination of rivers freed from long imprisonment.

I like to hope that my casting arm (and my wading legs) will hold up long enough that some day I can make a trip to the upper Elwha and try for steelhead as they pioneer their way back into a freshwater wilderness they've been denied for a century. If the fishes will be patient, maybe I can be, too.

CHAPTER SIX

OUTWORN
PRIVILEGES

*Trout Wonderland and the Institutionalizing
of Angling's Identity Crisis*

IN JULY OF 1873, THE NEW, AMBITIOUS LITTLE VILLAGE OF BOZEMAN,
Montana, was growing rapidly, but it was surrounded by country
that was still only partly known even to the people who lived there.
In the Yellowstone Valley, just twenty miles to the east, only a few
pioneers settled along the hundreds of miles of the Yellowstone
River across southern and eastern Montana Territory. Other now-
famous Yellowstone-area trout towns, including Livingston, Cody,
Jackson, and West Yellowstone, did not yet even exist.[1]

But the Yellowstone Valley was quickly being "discovered" by
Bozeman residents, who included both sportsmen and commercial hunters and fishermen. The first Bozeman newspaper, the
Avant Courier, watched with considerable anxiety as this discovery
went terribly wrong in the way that such early encounters with
abundant wildlife so often did:

We understand that measures are on foot to put an effec-
tual stop to the wholesale destruction of fish in the Yellowstone river by the use of seins, traps, &c. Those engaged in
this nefarious business had better desist. If a stop is not put
to it soon, by the time the valley is settled there will be no
fish in the stream, and those who enjoy the sport afforded
by the rod and line will have to angle a long while before
getting a bite.[2]

Today, the editor's indignation at such a slaughter seems not
only righteous but right. Most of us regard fish-hogs as fools. We
are appalled by the waste and disrespect of nature involved in wiping out wild animal populations, and offended at the tragically
short-sighted way those early Yellowstone River commercial fishermen went after that river's trout and whitefish.

But even today not all of us react that way. Each generation of
citizens has its share of people for whom such behavior is acceptable in some way. From the professional poacher to the unscrupu-
lous outfitter to the fisherman who just cheats on the regulations
now and then, such moral, social, and legal lapses live on. Perhaps
the big difference between now and then is that it used to be easier to get away with it.

Though the *Avant Courier* editorial does indicate that things
were changing, the greater historical picture of the times shows
that it was changing very slowly. Reading the papers and other
publications of those days we find the same diversity of opinion
on such matters that we find today. Some people were gleefully
wiping out the fish and game. Others were helplessly regretting
the waste and loss. But others, probably most others in fact, didn't
even care.[3]

Luckily, a few were mobilizing to prevent further slaughter, and eventually they would win out. But they faced an uphill and often thankless task in doing so. And, indeed, we still don't thank them enough. We certainly don't do enough to honor their memory, considering all they did to save wild animals and wild places for us.[4]

The achievements of the generations of conservationists since that time have been extraordinary, and few of those achievements have paid larger dividends than what they have done to protect the Yellowstone Valley. Now commonly billed as the last major undammed river in the lower forty-eight states, the Yellowstone has been a great beacon and blessing to anglers for more than a century. Management of any great natural resource, especially one with as many uses as a river, tests our patience, our knowledge, and our wisdom. With the Yellowstone River, that test continues today, and shows no sign that it will ever end. And perhaps the most concentrated and demanding of the Yellowstone's tests have occurred near the upper end of the river, in the area now known as Yellowstone National Park.

TROUT COMMERCE

In the notoriously corrupt "Gilded Age" that followed the Civil War, the creation of Yellowstone National Park seems even yet to have been a rare case of the public's best long-term interests winning out. It is amazing that this great idea would pop up in the middle of so much graft and greed.[5]

But we now know that even though it was a great idea, it was anything but a simple one. For many years a fairy-tale creation myth of the park prevailed, in which a few high-minded citizens, most of them members of the famous Washburn Party of Yellowstone explorers of 1870, fought to save the park solely because it

An 1882 park concessioner's promotional brochure emphasized the fabulous numbers of trout available to tourist-anglers in Yellowstone.
NATIONAL PARK SERVICE,
YELLOWSTONE NATIONAL PARK.

was in the public interest. It made a nice story to tell around camp-fires, but it didn't really happen that way.[6]

It is true that there were people back then who simply believed in the protection of beauty and wonder, but human nature was not on vacation. Two years before the park was created, the Northern Pacific Railroad had already put its considerable financial and political weight behind the park idea. They favored the park because it would provide them with additional passengers for proposed lines through that part of the West, and their support is what made the creation of Yellowstone National Park possible.

One of those original high-minded citizens who campaigned for the park was Nathaniel Langford, who would soon become the park's first superintendent. This man now perfectly symbolizes the complexity of Yellowstone's creation. By all accounts, Langford had his generous moments, but it's probably more significant in Yellowstone history that he was quietly on the railroad's payroll all during the campaign to create the park—from 1870, when he helped explore the future park area, until 1872, when President Grant signed the Yellowstone Park Act.[7]

In short, Yellowstone was created for a combination of altruistic, greedy, hopeful, aesthetic, social, public-spirited, emotional, and economic reasons. It is difficult for historians today even to roughly sort out which of these motives ruled, but you can never go wrong by betting on the money.

Trout and fishing were a part of this complicated mix of motivations and enthusiasms from the very beginning. As I have pointed out in a previous book, *Cowboy Trout* (2006), early park promoters were quick to celebrate the outstanding fishing available in the Yellowstone area.[8] Trout would help pay the park's way in the region's economic scene, just as they do today.

THE YELLOWSTONE OPINION WARS

This recognition of economics and self-interest as a driving force in conservation applies directly and historically to Yellowstone. The people who cared about Yellowstone in the 1800s were as complex and divided in their opinions as we are today. And though I continue to believe that some fair percentage of Yellowstone's supporters and defenders were and are essentially altruistic, most of us do mix that altruism with a hearty brew of personal preference bordering on religious conviction.

But because each person's altruism is not necessarily the next person's altruism—what, after all, is the "best" way to care for

Yellowstone National Park's mission has been repeatedly "redefined" since the park was created in 1872. Originally managed solely to produce the highest possible number of fish for anglers, park waters, like the Madison River pictured here, are now appreciated for providing a broad array of aesthetic, recreational, educational, and scientific opportunities. AUTHOR PHOTO.

Yellowstone?—and because our preferences and convictions are even more forcefully dissimilar, Yellowstone will always sit somewhere in the middle of a great and turbulent stream of public opinion. It will therefore always be one of this country's most important forums for debates over natural resources.

Here's the hardest lesson for many of us to learn. We like to think that we can get Yellowstone "right." In our debates over the park's management, we tend to speak with an almost biblical finality, as if the big questions of park management can all be permanently settled and we won't ever have to check in on the place again except to keep the Coke machines stocked and the bathrooms cleaned.

Read the editorials and letters columns of the regional news-papers near the park. Pick a topic that relates to Yellowstone and the surrounding public lands: fire, wolves, grizzly bears, elk, winter use, fishing, motorized recreation, overcrowding, facility construc-tion, Native American historical priorities, energy development, hard-rock mining, logging, bioprospecting. The list is long, and the position-takers are forceful and loud. Experts are everywhere. Simple answers slosh across the landscape like sewage spills.

This self assurance, this supreme confidence, may be the only thing all of us share. We certainly don't share much in the way of opinions about what actually *is* the best way to run the park.

Yellowstone can change, and it can be changed, and someone will always want to change it. As society's values and knowledge evolve, Yellowstone evolves too. I've called this process "searching for Yellowstone," because we Americans seem always to be strug-gling to define and redefine the park, and because I think that this process, as painful and clumsy as it sometimes becomes, may be the most important thing the park offers human society.

Please understand that I do not say these things as if I believe that I am above this fray. Like everyone else, I also am quite sure that I know what Yellowstone is for, and what its management should accomplish. But I've studied the debates over Yellowstone long enough to recognize that if we stand back a little ways, and see those debates as a creative and potentially helpful process, we'll be better off.

And I know how hard it is to stand back, especially if one chooses to participate in the conversations about Yellowstone in any meaningful way. You don't have to get defamed, misrepre-sented, or just lied about very often before you turn up the heat. Yellowstone has inspired some of the greatest political, social, and scientific pissing contests in the history of American land management. We show no sign of wising up and looking for other ways to go about the search.

But search we must. Yellowstone never lets us rest on our laurels, or get too comfortable with our value judgments. If Yellowstone isn't making us think, and if it isn't reminding us of how much we disagree among ourselves, we're probably not paying close enough attention.

This has everything to do with fisheries management in the park. In fact, it makes Yellowstone one of the most interesting places in the whole world to watch if you want to understand yourself and your angling ancestors.

BEGINNING

When Yellowstone was created, very little thought was given to treating its wild animals differently than they were treated elsewhere. It was assumed that visitors could hunt and fish in order to feed themselves, and they routinely did. Commercial hunting and fishing were prohibited but not in the least prevented.[9]

By the time the park was eleven years old, it was obvious that this arrangement wasn't working. The same greedy scumbags who were slaughtering the trout in the Yellowstone River in 1873 were doing similarly catastrophic work all over the West. The same professional hide-hunters who were just then finishing off the great western bison herds were also killing Yellowstone elk and bison by the thousands. So in 1883, public outcry was finally heard, and hunting became illegal in Yellowstone.

Many people are surprised to learn that sportsmen led the fight to prohibit hunting in Yellowstone. These early sportsmen gave us a great example of just the kind of enlightened self-interest that should guide us today. They recognized that Yellowstone could serve as a *wildlife reservoir*—a term they used and promoted. These foresightful conservationists correctly and repeatedly argued that as long as the park's summer ranges and ungulate calving grounds were protected, the park could perpetually provide an annual migratory flow of animals to hunting lands in all directions beyond park boundaries. They were right, and though the practice of wildlife management in and around Yellowstone remains complicated and controversial today, the principle of the wildlife reservoir is proven beyond any doubt.[10]

Banning public hunting in Yellowstone National Park in 1883 was one of the key defining moments in the entire history of the American national park movement. Hardly anyone back then knew what it would all really mean, just as now very few people know it even happened, but what sportsmen achieved when they prohibited hunting in Yellowstone in 1883 was momentous. With one simple change in park regulations, they turned Yellowstone into the world's foremost wildlife reserve.

They also dramatically changed the nature of the park visit. Within a few years, the chance to observe the rare large mammals of North America became one of the primary reasons for visiting the park, as important to many tourists as seeing Old Faithful or the Grand Canyon of the Yellowstone.

What this also meant is that after 1883, fish were the only species of Yellowstone animal still available for direct public sport and consumption. That made them a very special resource, one that, in the minds of most people who thought about such things back then, needed further "development." When Euroamericans arrived in the Yellowstone region in the early 1800s, 40 percent of the park's area was without fish of any sort, including almost all of

Yellowstone fishing has changed much since the days of the barbaric and popular practice among early park visitors who captured trout in Yellowstone Lake and then cooked them while alive in the famous "Fishing Cone" hot spring at West Thumb Geyser Basin. FROM FERDINAND HAYDEN, *SIXTH ANNUAL REPORT OF THE UNITED STATES GEOLOGICAL AND GEOGRAPHICAL SURVEY OF THE TERRITORIES* (1873).

the Firehole River, and both Lewis and Shoshone Lakes. In 1889, in one of my all-time favorite Yellowstone quotes that I repeat every chance I get, no less famous an angler and tourist than Rudyard Kipling described the Firehole River as "a warm and deadly river wherein no fish breed."[11]

Everybody knows how quickly that changed. Between 1886 and 1920, almost all park waters were stocked with fish. The goal was to create the best possible fishing, and early managers were amazingly successful. Even in the 1890s, Yellowstone was internationally famous for its fishing, which, like wildlife watching, became a permanent and primary attraction for tourists.[12]

PUBLIC WILL AND SPECIAL INTERESTS

As visitation increased, so did fishing pressure. Creel limits were gradually reduced, but surprisingly early in the park's history the quality of the fishing began to fail. As John Varley and I pointed out in our book *Yellowstone Fishes: Ecology, History, and Angling in the Park* (1999), by 1920 it was obvious that the fishing was getting poorer.[13] Like too many sportsmen even today, anglers were reluctant to blame themselves; many people blamed the poor fishing on predation of fish by gulls, pelicans, and other animals, and simply ignored the effects of increasing numbers of human anglers. We just weren't ready to accept our own role in a problem like this.

But more was changing than the quality of the fishing. After the National Park Service was created in 1916, it became easier for conservationists to observe the trend of management in all the parks. As more parks were created, more people, with more diverse interests, began to pay attention. Fishermen were no longer the only people interested in Yellowstone's aquatic ecosystems, and some of the other people didn't even approve of fishing.

There's a historical reality here that requires emphasizing. National Park Service fishing policy, like other policies, is not something cooked up in each individual park. Among the criticisms that I hear and read of the Yellowstone region's federal agencies—National Park Service, U.S. Forest Service, U.S. Fish and Wildlife Service, Bureau of Land Management—the most common misconception is that the local managers just independently dreamed up a new policy one day.

(I know why this happens, by the way. It happens because it is more satisfying to personalize these changes in public land policy, and to be able to blame specific individuals. The first effective step in aggressive public debate these days is to diminish and demonize your opponent, and you can't do that without identifying that opponent. Put a face on evil and you're on your way. Federal bureaucrats are the handiest of targets, and in the West there is a long tradition of recklessly attacking them. If you're ambitious for elected office in the West, you can hardly go wrong by trashing the feds.)

Federal land-management policy, at least big important policy, isn't created that simply. Even Yellowstone, which has often had a leadership role in the development of policy in the national park system, is responding to a complex set of legislative mandates and an equally complex set of national public attitudes.

Park policies are, in fact, a reflection of public will, and they even tend to lag behind that will. That doesn't mean that we have to like those policies, but it does mean we have to pay attention to the national mood from which they grew.

Public will is inevitably a difficult thing to gauge, because the public is well known for never having a unanimous opinion. Routinely, special interest groups concerned about natural-resource management, wherever they fall on the political spectrum, tend to use the rhetoric common among activists in the 1960s—they claim that they represent and speak for "the people." In fact, special interest groups only represent their memberships. Or at least the memberships hope so.

Like it or not, we fishermen are a special interest group. We are naturally convinced that our interest is *unusually* special, but when viewed from the outside, by an observer watching the interplay of many such interest groups, we are probably indistinguishable from the others. We would have a hard time proving that we really represent the interests of "the people" any more than do other groups.

ALIENS

In the complicated matter of the special interests of anglers in Yellowstone, especially how those interests may change over the long haul, consider the example of non-native fish species in national parks. For nearly a century now, many conservationists and scientists have expressed concern over the widespread distribution of non-native fish in national parks. Yellowstone managers became concerned about threats that non-native fish posed to the park experience and to native fish species a surprisingly long time ago, and stopped introducing new species before 1910. But by then, a full array of non-natives were already present, and their presence has complicated management ever since.

The gradual change in natural-resource management represented by Yellowstone's reluctance to accept any more non-native species reflected important societal changes. In 1920, the American Association for the Advancement of Science, the leading scientific society in the western hemisphere, formally resolved to oppose any additional introductions of any exotic species, plant or animal, to any national park. The Ecological Society of America adopted a similar resolution the same year. In 1925, Dr. Charles Adams, one of the founders of the modern scientific discipline of ecology and director of the distinguished Roosevelt Wild Life Forest Experiment Station of Syracuse University, articulated the power of this concern for the protection of native aquatic ecosystems in national parks. His words should have served as an early warning to anglers that they were no longer alone among the public in their interest in fish:

> The idea that forests with big game animals should be
> maintained as a wilderness, and that there is an advantage

in natural wild waters, appears to be a new conception for our parks. Some of the same persons who are very eager to maintain a wilderness for certain purposes have never recognized that others are equally interested in an untouched aquatic wilderness.[14]

Let's keep in mind who these people were. This was a significant element of the scientific establishment speaking. We're not talking about some fringe group of extremists here. Nor are we talking about the superintendent of Yellowstone, who at the time would probably have even taken an opposing position. Science was right then flexing its muscles and would soon cross the line from being a special interest group to being an integral part of park management decision-making. The scientific community demonstrated the enormous damage that can be done to aquatic ecosystems by the introduction of non-native species. National Park Service policy has come to reflect that scientific certainty much more strongly than it used to, in parks all over the country.[15]

Restoration of native species is a real emotional sizzler for a lot of anglers these days because it threatens, or seems to threaten, the established order of things on a lot of streams now inhabited by thriving, robust populations of non-native trout that—along with their anglers and managers—are being cast as bad guys in a global ecological drama.[16]

But native species restoration has a grand and heroic ring to the general public, and for good reason. We as a nation decided a long time ago that we believe in this sort of thing. In our typical can-do fashion, we Americans brought back the bald eagle and the bison, the trumpeter swan and the elk. Attempts to restore other "glamour animals," such as the whooping crane and the California condor, are widely heralded as important conservation sagas. Buy the poster, wear the T-shirt.

Go to any big fisheries-research or conservation symposium to witness the results of this powerful movement. There will be heart-wrenching presentations about this or that relict fish population—some rare little biological jewel that is barely hanging on in a few remote headwaters of its once extensive range. When pictures of these little fish appear on the screen, the sense of hopeful urgency in the room is almost palpable. Creatures like these are well on their way to becoming the new symbols of the conservation movement. They have the law on their side. And because so many parts of the country have at least one or two of these imperiled little guys swimming around in the local watersheds, native fish conservation is a growth industry in management circles as well as in the larger conservation community of which anglers are only a small part.

If that isn't enough turmoil for us, generations of angling writers, naturalists, and artists have devoted themselves to portraying the beauty and value of wild native fish. Having set ourselves up like that, we shouldn't be surprised when the non-angling conservationists laugh or shake their heads in disgust when they hear that anglers often resist such restorations because we'd rather fish for the exotic fish species that replaced the natives. Relative sporting qualities of the species in question is not a very persuasive issue with a lot of people in the new generation of conservationists. Right or wrong, like it or not, when anglers fight against native fish restoration, we look selfishly out of date, and our high-flown talk of ethics is unconvincing, especially in a place like Yellowstone National Park, where the world knows that native species and native ecosystems have become a central point of bothering to preserve the place at all.

This gets worse. The whole restoration industry now flourishing among natural resource managers exists to fix problems we caused. Non-angling conservationists are quick to point out that it was us, or the fisheries managers we hired, who introduced all those non-native animal species in the first place (recall the tailwaters in the previous chapter). They then point out that when we dumped all those exotics in the water, we destroyed a host of so-called "undesirable species."

Past actions (call them "mistakes" if you want; everybody else does) in wildlife management are a part of the American sporting legacy that our critics most like to focus public attention on. The sins of the fathers will haunt us forever. Yellowstone's mixing bowl of native and non-native species, as wonderful as the fishing is, and as beautiful as the fish are, is a monument to earlier good intentions gone awry.

WILDNESS AND ANGLING

Still, things have worked pretty well for anglers in Yellowstone. Most of the time, the National Park Service's mandate to preserve native ecosystems actually worked to the advantage of good fishing. Preserving wildness, after all, is a pretty good way of preserving wild trout.

We saw this dovetailing of interests work especially well in Yellowstone starting in the 1960s. The decline in fishing that was noted as early as the 1920s had continued for decades. Despite intensive management efforts, fishing went downhill in the 1930s, 1940s, and 1950s.

Some positive steps were taken over those decades, often to the advantage of native species even though mostly aimed at trying to prop up the sport fishery. Managers, responding to a growing public interest in wild trout, closed the park's last hatcheries in the 1950s.[17] But the most dramatic changes didn't come until the late 1960s, under the administration of Superintendent Jack Anderson.

Many of us, especially those of us who were fishing in the early 1970s, recall the revolution in fisheries management that occurred in the park, and in Montana. The rise of widespread catch-and-release fishing regulations, the discovery and loud announcement of the harmful effects of hatchery fish on wild fish, and the institution of other special regulations, all led to a gratifying improvement in the quality of the fishing in Yellowstone that lasted until the more recent arrival of illegally introduced lake trout in Yellowstone Lake, and the even more recent arrival of whirling disease and other exotic problems.

Because of its unusual jurisdictional independence (the park was created before any of the surrounding states and thus enjoys exclusive jurisdiction in its land-management operations), Yellowstone National Park was able to move faster and more decisively in revising outdated fishing regulations than were most other national parks or states. But similar programs have slowly prevailed in many other places. The changes were in good part the result of the changing will of the people, especially the people who cared most about fish. Without the strong support of anglers as represented by their special interest groups—the Federation of Fly Fishers, Trout Unlimited, Theodore Gordon Fly Fishers, and many other organized fishermen and fisheries professionals—it probably couldn't have happened.

It's true, though, that not all anglers favored these changes. Most of those who preferred bait-fishing and catch-and-kill, as well as the people who don't really care what species of fish are in

Long thought safe from "civilization" because of its legislative protection, Yellowstone National Park now demonstrates the fragility of all wild aquatic ecosystems in the face of invasive species. In 1989, Wyoming angler Wendy Baylor easily captured large cutthroat trout from this backcountry tributary of Pelican Creek in east-central Yellowstone. In less than two decades, whirling disease and lake trout (illegally introduced into Yellowstone Lake, to which Pelican Creek is a primary tributary) have virtually eliminated such trout from the entire Pelican Creek system. AUTHOR PHOTO.

park streams as long as there are lots of them, probably did not change their minds. They just gradually became a less significant part of the park's fisheries constituency. They were left behind, as they were on other public waters where less consumptive fisheries regulations took hold. The old-school bait-fishers and fish-harvesters were part of angling's long and honorable tradition, but their methods just didn't fit in the park anymore, so they either adjusted to the new regulations or transferred their recreational allegiances to other waters outside the park, most of which were still managed in traditional ways.

For about seventy years, the public flocked to Fishing Bridge, at the outlet to Yellowstone Lake, for the park's most freewheeling social fishing scene. The bridge was closed to fishing in 1973, as part of a modernization of fishing regulations throughout the park, to protect spawning trout. NATIONAL PARK SERVICE PHOTOGRAPH, YELLOWSTONE NATIONAL PARK.

I suspect that Yellowstone's fishermen may eventually look back on that period of the 1970s and 1980s as the last time when we could really feel that we had the public will so strongly on our side.

THE NEW AGE

Even in the 1960s, there were signs of an uneasy future. In the mid-sixties, the Conservation Foundation commissioned two leading ecologists, F. Fraser Darling and Noel Eichhorn, to study the national parks and report on their prospects. In the influential book *Man and Nature in the National Parks*, which I have often quoted as a significant indicator of changing American values relating to wild places and wild animals, Darling and Eichhorn said, "Fishing, surely, is one of those outworn privileges in a national park of the later 20th Century."[18]

My copy of the Darling and Eichhorn book contains many of my peevish marginal notations, in which I point out to myself just how poorly these two authors understood fishing, either as a sport or as the passion of a significant political constituency. It's very easy to lose ourselves in anger or indignation when someone speaks so absolutely against us and with so little apparent understanding of what we do. But these views are not going to go away. They are going to become more widespread. So let's make sure we understand them.

The most important thing to recognize about the Darling and Eichhorn view, which many people hold today, is that they expressed no moral objection to fishing. Just as many of us in the 1960s and 1970s saw that bait-fishing no longer belonged in the park, these non-fisherfolk believed that *no anglers at all* belong in the park. They believed that the parks had evolved into a new kind of reserve, where nature was best enjoyed less consumptively than in most other places. Fishing did not seem to them to fit the new mold, any more than did public bear-feeding grounds and other old-time park activities that were being phased out at the same time. I'm confident that many more people would agree with Darling and Eichhorn today than might have in the 1960s. We who love to fish in the park need to recognize that their argument has considerable intellectual heft and growing social momentum.

But as we all know, there are also people with moral objections to fishing. We who hunt have been hearing from these people for a long time. Actually, I'm surprised that so far, the moralistic attacks on fishing in the parks have been so poorly articulated and weakly executed. I thought those attacks would have intensified far more than they have by now. But based on its history of attracting controversy, I still imagine that Yellowstone will eventually be a leading site for this debate. Any organization with any media savvy at all knows that you stand a better chance of making headlines here than you do in almost any other natural area in the United States.

As I will further suggest in the next chapter, the animal-rights and animal-welfare movements are several centuries old. Many if not most of the modern arguments were worked out and vigorously exercised hundreds of years ago, no matter how "new" the movement may seem to some of us today. The difference between the movement one hundred years ago and now may be largely demographic. As a larger and larger percentage of the public moved to the cities and suburbs, and were divorced from direct contact with wild nature, a larger percentage of them became removed from the need to use and interact with those animals in traditional ways, and could adopt moral stances that were beyond their reach, if not beyond their comprehension, two hundred or even one hundred years earlier.

Animal rights has an interesting history in Yellowstone, too. It hasn't been that long ago that those of us who watched the public debates over Yellowstone's management could view the more extreme elements of the animal rights movement almost as a joke. But as Yellowstone's staff has learned in the past twenty or thirty years, the leadership of the animal rights groups have developed daunting technical and political skills, and now are among the major voices in dialogues over the management of the park.

They are not only vocal. They are numerous. When Yellowstone's managers narrowed the scope of fishing opportunities in

Yellowstone with modern special regulations, they also narrowed the constituency that had a personal stake in the perpetuation of fishing in the park, at a time when opponents to the sport appear to be increasing in number.

TODAY

At issue in Yellowstone today is much more than what the current set of bureaucrats in the park are trying to accomplish in honoring their legislative mandates. At issue are fundamental changes in the way Americans view nature. Scientific disciplines that didn't exist professionally just fifty years ago, such as conservation biology and landscape ecology, are changing the way conservation professionals and advocates view the resources of national parks. These disciplines inform the positions of many scientific societies and conservation groups, including angling groups and people who regard angling as inappropriate to the park mission. They also are adopted and adapted to the openly moral agendas of other interest groups.

One thing has not changed in the history of all this. Most people who regard fishing as inappropriate in parks, for whatever reason, have a weak or at least incomplete grasp of what sport is all about, much less of what sport fishing in a national park can do for public appreciation of nature. But many of their arguments are sound enough, and politically appealing enough, that we should be listening carefully. Whether they are right or wrong isn't the point. The point is that they're here, and they are players in the modern dialogues over how parks should be managed.

Most of us are reasonably sure that fishing will be going on in the national parks for a long time yet. There really haven't been any forceful legal or political challenges to the appropriateness of fishing in national parks. But at the same time we must recognize that the mission of the national parks is complex and has evolved, and that fishing as a park activity must be made to fit into the greater mandate to protect wild native ecosystems.

In the history of Yellowstone, it has become progressively more difficult to eliminate a traditional, well-established use as the park has grown older. I think American society will have to change its values a lot more before fishing is really threatened in the parks.

As comforting as we may find that, we cannot always count on the long, slow haul of history to drag things out. Thirty years ago, I doubt that more than a few British citizens would have dreamed that the ancient, tradition-rich, and well-funded sport of fox hunting could abruptly be banished from the entire nation.[19] When certain social and political thresholds are crossed, things can change fast, and it is very hard to know just when we are approaching such a threshold.

Whether fishing thrives in the Yellowstone of the future is mostly going to depend upon how successful we sportsmen are at adapting and keeping pace with the complicated changes in society's idea of nature, and at educating "the people" in the value of the fishing experience in national parks.

It may be an uneasy future for Yellowstone anglers, but this is another instance that some uneasiness is good for us. The sort of complacency and overconfidence that led early Yellowstone anglers to take the fishery for granted and even to presume they were exempt from any blame for its declining health hasn't really disappeared. We're just as complacent about other things, including the presumed rightness of our values as sportsmen, and our disregard for the way our activities may impinge on the values of others.

Complacency won't work here. Yellowstone isn't an institution that rewards ingrown thinking. We anglers have so much going for us along the streams and lakes of the park that we should welcome the tough questions that Yellowstone will continue to ask us.

CHAPTER SEVEN

IF FISH
COULD SCREAM

*How Cruelty Helped Shape
the Modern Fly Fisher*

A RECENT SUNDAY EPISODE OF THE COMIC STRIP "DILBERT" featured the hilarious Machiavellian dog character, Dogbert, conducting a "Catch-And-Release CEO Seminar," in which he explained to his audience that "catch-and-release is more than a way to hurt fish for entertainment. It's a philosophy that will inform your entire life."[1] This and other attacks on catch-and-release fishing by Dilbert's characters are an indication of an issue emerging from the obscurity of a specialty into the harsh light of broader public interest. Such emergence is often a good thing, but it is never a simple thing. Specialists of every sort have learned the hard way that once endorsement or disapproval of you hits the funny papers, you're in the hands of popular culture and the stakes have just gotten a lot higher.

Though all sport fishers are under fire from one segment of the animal-rights community or another, fly fishing inspires a special outrage among opponents of fishing because fly fishers have so eagerly embraced catch-and-release fishing. Catch-and-release is not an especially new idea in fisheries management circles, but its popularization in recent decades has been one of those sea changes that occasionally sweeps through a human pursuit and requires decades of debate and rumination before we come to terms with it—or just get used to it and find something more pressing to argue about.

Catch-and-release anglers face especially increasing criticism from people who object to the apparent cruelty of fishing not for food but for "mere sport." Even some people with no strong moral objection to catching fish for both sport *and* food are troubled by catch-and-release, which they see as crossing some line between acceptable sporting behavior and callous disregard for the wild animal.

Likewise, it appears that many anglers feel the same way and insist that they will only fish for food and will stop fishing as soon as they have enough. Read, for one example of many, John McPhee's entertaining, literate, and heated anti-catch-and-release rant in *The Founding Fish* (2002) to discover just how strongly even fishermen can disagree over this matter—as well as to discover that even a brilliant journalist can be as judgmental and inflexible as the rest of us when he cuts loose.[2]

McPhee is firmly in the camp of those who believe that the only morally justifiable reason for catching fish is to kill them and eat them. He also believes that this is not a negotiable matter, and anyone who differs with him is doing something very wrong. He is, in this respect, the type specimen of catch-and-release disputants. Every point on the spectrum of convictions is problematic from most other points on the spectrum.

Whatever position you hold on this spectrum, if you're listening carefully to your critics you may recognize the thin line between the glib cheap shot and the genuinely penetrating criticism. It is, for example, both glib and penetrating to point out that proponents of catching fish only if you're going to kill them are in the odd position of seeming to prefer the death of the fish, while the catch-and-release angler they vilify prefers the fish to live. Who, we might ask, cares more about the fish?

Here the glib and the penetrating intertwine almost inseparably. No doubt the fish, in the net or hand of a given angler, would vote to be released. But no doubt the fish would also vote not to have been caught in the first place, and that is the point made by the critics. They insist that unless you're going to kill and eat it, you shouldn't catch it in the first place. For the catch-and-kill anglers, the intention to release entirely defeats the point of catching.[3] Surviving unbothered until unfortunate enough to be caught by a fish killer is, by this line of reasoning, the fish's best choice.

Some introduce other complicated ideas into the conversation at this point, saying that catch-and-release is more disrespectful to the fish, or at least is more of a compromise of the fish's dignity as a wild animal. I agree that all species of animals deserve our respect, and I favor the notion that many species of animal do have an inherent dignity. But I suspect that most people who apply such terms to wild animals are more concerned with projecting their own idea of those concepts onto other animals than they are really trying to sort out how such things might work in the animals' own world. Neither the catch-and-kill nor the catch-and-release angler is putting the fish's interests above their own. The fish is still the less important creature.

Most of us who fish don't trouble ourselves with these questions much anyway. The fish's needs are important to us only insofar as *we* need them for this whole sport to work in the first place. We judge our needs as more important than those of the fish, and no matter how simple our needs seem to our critics, our needs are in fact very complicated.

So is sport. As I have elsewhere suggested, sport is one of those ancient human endeavors—like music, storytelling, cuisine, painting, war, architecture, and religion—that has caused us no end of thought, delight, and consternation as long as human culture has existed. To trivialize sport as "mere" is, first, to admit that one is embarrassingly ignorant of what's going on in this particular human endeavor and, second, to cheapen a dialogue that deserves to be conducted with a good deal more mutual respect and accurate information.[4]

Our deliberations about fishing are about what is right for us—not only what is right for us as sportsmen, but what is right for us in our relationship with the natural world. As I say, I wouldn't for a minute suggest that most sportsmen give this lofty inquiry much thought on a day-to-day basis, but cumulatively what we do out there on the water—the values we exercise and the decisions we make—shapes tomorrow's sporting culture as surely as if such challenging issues were on our minds all the time.

Catch-and-release fishing is just one example of this powerful yet diffuse process by which sport gets defined and redefined.[5] I introduce the catch-and-release debate here mostly because it's such a lively topic and because it provides the perfect opening to look at how the bigger questions behind it have played out in making fly fishers who they are.

WISHFUL THINKING PAID OFF

Lately, catch-and-release anglers, long plagued by these accusations of sadistic cruelty, are enjoying some comfort in the findings of a scientific paper by Dr. James Rose, "The Neurobehavioral Nature of Fishes and the Question of Awareness and Pain," published in *Reviews in Fisheries Science* in 2002. Dr. Rose has argued that fish lack the necessary biological equipment to feel pain or experience awareness as humans understand those terms.[6]

The great thing about science is that the jury is permanently out. There is always more to be learned and often something to be unlearned as well. But as scientific arguments go, Dr. Rose's case is indeed well made and justifies the present confidence of anglers. It is never safe to feel secure, much less smug, when one has opponents as intelligent, determined, and politically adept as the animal rights crowd, but maybe it's okay for catch-and-release fishermen to be a little relieved about how the debate over whether fish feel pain is going these days.

As well, maybe all those fishermen who, for many generations now, have been hopefully claiming that fish don't feel pain were just engaging in arrogant, self-serving guesswork and wishful thinking, but it looks like they were at least guessing and thinking in the right direction. Lucky guess or not, you get credit when you're right.

Still, even if every relevant scientific authority on fish neurobiology suddenly stood up and agreed with Dr. Rose, the greater social and moral issues would not go away, and—holding to my skeptical theme in previous chapters—I'm not sure we fishermen should want them to. Nothing breeds complacency like overconfidence, and five minutes on the website of the People for the Ethical Treatment of Animals should convince any of us that we anglers surely can't afford either overconfidence or complacency.

In the long view of these debates over the cruelty of fishing, however, there is something else important about Dr. Rose's work. What he is telling us might be called new. Recent science appears to have clarified previously unknown aspects of fish neurobiology. This is certainly helpful for what it contributes to society's dialogue over cruelty and pain in fishing, but it is also significant because in the long history of that dialogue, most of the important arguments were made long ago and each new generation of disputants just repeated them with new rhetorical trimmings. There's rarely some new big thing to add to the conversation.

As interesting and important as the debate over catch-and-release fishing is these days, it is only one heated expression of much older moral and ethical struggles that we anglers have alternately engaged and evaded for centuries. The pain and cruelty that we are accused of inflicting upon fish are much more than just old stories; they were fundamental to the creation of modern fly fishing.

ANCIENT PAIN

Human bewilderment over just where we fit in the animal world, how other species of animals fit in our world, and how we should all get along in the same world is one of our most ancient dilemmas as thinking beings. As one historical scholar has put it, "All human cultures studied by anthropologists face the problem that they are both animal and not-animal."[7] Though most anglers and anti-anglers seem ignorant of it, there is a large, venerable litera-

For as long as anglers have celebrated their sport as an innocent and wholesome pastime, other observers have taken a darker view of the whole enterprise. COURTESY OF THE AMERICAN MUSEUM OF FLY FISHING.

ture devoted to the complications and quandaries of human relationships with other animals. Most of this literature, especially before the late 1800s and the emergence of wildlife conservation as a public concern, was devoted to concerns over domestic animals. What concerns there were about wild animals were almost entirely concentrated on warm-blooded species.

In the 1500s, the majority of the British public still enjoyed a variety of what we now would consider hideously vicious activities relating to animals. Many loved such barbaric spectacles as bear baiting—forcing fights between dogs and bears, a recreation that offended people as much for the cruelty it inspired between the animals as for any inherent unkindness on the part of the humans who arranged the fights. Even more shocking, many people found some incomprehensible satisfaction in cat burning, which was accomplished in a variety of ways, apparently just for the excitement of hearing the cats scream. Whatever moral force the people who opposed these recreations exercised was lost in the general enthusiasm of all the people who enjoyed them.[8]

To modern sensitivities, these types of cruelty are almost as shocking for the inventiveness of their methods as for their heartless disregard of the animal's agony. Only three or four centuries ago in England, if an especially hated person was being burned in effigy, some cats might be lashed inside the stuffed dummy, so that it would seem to emit screams as it burned.[9]

Among domestic animals, treatment of working livestock was more often at the heart of early criticisms of cruelty to animals. In 1610, the writer of rural manuals Gervase Markham objected to the "tyrannical martyring of poor horses" that were routinely and violently broken, overworked, and whipped.[10] Human society had a vague generalized conscience when it came to other species of animals, but most individual humans didn't seem to worry much about whatever pangs they might have felt, and the common conscience was generally unaffected or suppressed.

CHEATERS

For most of the documented history of the animal rights and anti-cruelty movements, fish were given short shrift. Comparatively speaking, they still are. Bioethicist Peter Singer's milestone book, *Animal Liberation: A New Ethics for Our Treatment of Animals* (1975), for a generation the foremost popular manual for animal rights advocates, devoted less than five of 297 pages to fish, and those five

For centuries, writers on sport have debated the relative merits and even the morality of the various blood sports, but most early anglers would have seen little reason to differentiate themselves from other harvesters of wild food sources. The angler pictured in Leonard Mascall's *A Book of Engines and Traps* (1590) engaged the natural world no differently than did the trapper across the stream setting a snare on an animal trail. Each of these activities might be perceived by its practitioners as both "sport and pastime," and each would be repeatedly critiqued and condemned on the grounds of cruelty.

A
Booke of Engines
and traps to take Polcats,
Buzardes, Rattes, Mice and all
other kindes of Vermine and beasts what-
foeuer, moſt profitable for all Warri-
ners, and ſuch as delight in this
kinde of ſport and
paſtime.

LONDON
Printed by Iohn Wolfe, and are to be ſold
by Edward White dwelling at the little North
doze of Paules at the ſigne of the Gunne.
1590.

pages were notably superficial in their treatment of the complex issues of human-fish relations.[11] Despite recently increased emphasis on fish among animal-rights groups, this imbalance prevails today among the public, in good part because fish are so much less like us than are brown-eyed, warm-blooded creatures. We just don't relate to fish very well, any more than we relate well to snakes or insects.

For some centuries our emotional distancing from other animals was also a matter of necessity. Anything we have ever *needed* to hurt or eat wasn't going to get a lot of abstract sympathy from us, if it even occurred to us that such sympathy might be deserved. Medieval Christians, depending upon their role in the church, may have had as many as 150 days each year when they were not allowed to consume mammal flesh.[12] Some other animals had to fill in, and fish did. Sympathy for them surely must have seemed a luxury.

This is not to say that nobody paid any attention to the moral complications of our treatment of fish. There is little or no way of knowing what all those illiterate medieval souls who tended their local stew ponds and netted their local waters for centuries may have thought about killing so many essentially defenseless creatures, or if they thought of it at all. But it takes only one reasonably old example of criticism of angling to suggest just how troubling even fishing for food seemed to some people a few hundred years ago.

In 1646, Dr. Martin Lluelyn, a Welsh poet, parson, and physician, published a poem, "A Song Against Fishing." Lluelyn found fault with fishing on several levels. Let's try one of his verses:

> He that searches Pooles and Dikes,
> Halters Jackes and strangles Pikes,
> Let him know, though he thinke he wise is,
> 'Tis not a sport but an Assizes.
> Fish so tooke, were the case disputed,
> Are not tooke, but executed.
> Breake thy Rod about thy Noddle,
> Through thy wormes and flies by the Pottle,
> Keepe thy Corke to stoppe thy Bottle,
> Make straight thy hooke, and be not afeard,

> *To shave his Beard;*
> *That in case of started stitches,*
> *Hooke and Line may mend the Britches.*[13]

A little translation might help. "Jackes" would most likely have referred to small pike or other fish. "Assizes" usually referred to court proceedings, but in this context it referred more specifically to a court edict of death. "Noddle" meant "head." "Through" was almost certainly "throw," and "Pottle" was a two-quart drinking vessel, but this statement about throwing worms and flies is still somewhat obscure. It at least meant discarding worm and bait. A hook's "beard" would have been the barb, and "started stitches" would have been loose or pulled stitches in an item of clothing that required mending.

So far, the message of Lluelyn's poem was clear: killing fish was very nearly murder no matter how you did it, and you should convert all your tackle to good domestic tools.

But let's consider another of Lluelyn's verses:

> *But of all men he is the Cheater,*
> *Who with small fish takes up the Greater,*
> *He makes Carpes without all dudgen*
> *Make a Jonas of a Gudgeon.*
> *Cruell man that slayes on Gravell*
> *Fish that Great with Fish doth Travell.*[14]

Here other issues surfaced. First, we are confronted with one of the most significant distinctions between hunting and fishing. Hunting required you to kill some animal independent of its own impulses, as in stalking a deer or flushing a grouse while those animals are either unaware of you or are trying to escape from you. By contrast, fishing required you to persuade your quarry to attack and kill something else (your bait, your fly, your lure) so that you could thereby deceive and kill it.

For Lluelyn this form of deception amounted to moral treachery, at least when live bait was used. The fisherman was a "cheater" because he used a small fish for bait to capture a larger fish. Rather as some people of this period disapproved of bringing out the cruelty in the dogs used in bear-baiting (as mentioned above), Lluelyn disliked our appealing to the violent impulses of the larger fish—the carp attacks and eats the little gudgeon (just as the whale ate Jonah). The angler thereby made the bait fish his unwilling but culpable accomplice in an act of deceit.

But there was more to the angler's immorality. He also took unfair advantage of spawning fish (fish that were "great" with their young). Here was an element of sporting manners or ethics that eventually made its way into fly fishing's modern ethical stance. In most circumstances, catching fish while they are vulnerable on shallow spawning beds (on "Gravell") is now regarded as unsporting because it takes unfair advantage of unusually catchable fish.[15]

In the course of these and other verses, Lluelyn dismissed fishing comprehensively as an immoral activity, full of deceit and unfair death-dealing.

But here is the big surprise for the modern reader. In the whole poem there was not a word about the cruelty of causing a fish pain. Both fishing and the people who questioned the values behind it were much more complicated than we might have imagined.

WITHOUT HURTING HIM

When pain did surface in the early fishing literature, it was likewise a complicated matter. Judging from the very modest sample
of comments that we are provided by the small number of
sixteenth- and seventeenth-century fishing books, early critics of
fishing, as well as those people who loved fishing and were hoping to elevate its moral stance, were not noticeably concerned
with possible cruelty to the fish they were trying to catch. Instead,
the cruelty that worried these people was cruelty toward the *bait*.
Just as Lluelyn was unhappy about how fishing required us to
appeal to the basest instincts of big fish who wanted to eat little
fish, others were concerned about the cruelty of using live creatures for bait at all.

To appreciate this seemingly strange twist in the story, it is
necessary to review some of the early fishing books. Even recognizing that a lot of bait fishermen today do things not all that dissimilar from what these anglers were doing 400 or 500 years ago,
it's still easy to be shocked by these texts. If you've spent as much
time fly fishing as I have, and have gotten some emotional distance on your bait-fishing upbringing—or if you've never been
involved in bait fishing in the first place—this stuff reads like a
Starter Manual for Young Sadists.

Some of it at least had the advantage of being brief. Leonard
Mascall's *A Booke of Fishing with Hooke & Line* (1590), contained
basic bait instructions for "quicke baites," by which he meant live
baits.[16] These included "young frogges, the feete cut off by the
body or by the knee,"[17] and "also the grasse-hopper, his legges and
winges [cut off] by the body."[18] Ironically, Gervase Markham,
mentioned earlier for his outrage over the brutal mistreatment of

of wood made thinne and flatte : put it in at the gille, betwixt the skinne and the bodie of the Roch, and so forth at the taile, and drawe your armed wiar and hooke after, and place your hooke close vnder his gill, and so dragge for him as ye doe for the Darce. If it bee with a single hooke you shall put in your armed wiar at the mouth of the Roch or Gogin, and it will serue well enough, as ye may here see by figure, there is to drag with a liue Frogge, and tie the double hooke vnder his necke and hippes.

The single hooke.

The double hooke vnder the gill.

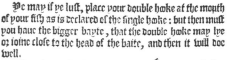

The armed hooke

Ye may if ye lust, place your double hooke at the mouth of your fish as is declared of the single hooke : but then must you haue the bigger bayte, that the double hooke may lye or ioine close to the head of the baite, and then it will doe well.

There is another kinde of hooke, calde a proching hooke, which is made without a barke, this kinde or manner of hookes

The earliest published criticisms of "cruel" fishermen often focused on the inhumane treatment of the bait—small fish, frogs, and other animals whose living bodies were mutilated and threaded through with lines and hardware. Anglers were also accused of further injuring these small animals so their struggles and bleeding would heighten their appeal as bait. Typical of these proceedings was a woodcut engraving of a live-bait rigging method from Leonard Mascall, *A Booke of Fishing with Hooke & Line* (1590).

horses, gave this same advice about mutilating live frogs and grasshoppers in his *The Pleasures of Princes* (1614).[19]

But later in the seventeenth century there appeared much more fulsome and gruesome guidance on how to prepare baits. Here's James Chetham, writing in 1689 on how to rig a perch or frog for pike fishing. Make sure you follow this closely, to get the full effect of what's being done to these little animals.

. . . Though the Pearch be the worst Bait, yet he'll live longest on the Hook; and is to be baited thus, *viz*, having cutt off his Fin on his Back without hurting him, with a sharp Knife, betwixt the head and the Fin on the Back, cut or make an Incision, or such a Scar as you may put the arming Wire of your Hook into it, with as little bruising or hurting of the Fish as possible, and so carrying your arming Wire a-long his back, into or near the Tail of your Fish, betwixt the Skin and the body of it, draw out the Wire or Arming of your Hook at another Scar near to his Tail, then tye him about it with Thread, but no harder than of necessity to prevent hurting the Fish. And some use a kind of Probe to open the way, for the more easy entrance or passage of your Arming or Wire: And thus bait your ledger Bait for Pike, and keep it a foot from the bottom; for a Pike will not so soon take any Bait on the Ground, as if it swim about a foot or more from the bottom.

To bait a Frog for the Pike do it thus; *viz*, put your arming Wire in at his Mouth (which you may do betwixt *May*-day and the end of *August*; for afterwards his Mouth closes up) and out at his Guills, and then, with a fine Needle and Silk, sow the upper part of his Leg with only one stitch to the arming Wire, or tye the Frogs Leg to the upper joint of the Wire. Use him gentley, and perform your operation neatly, and he'll live the longer on your Hook.[20]

When Chetham instructed readers to perform these various surgeries on the bait animal's body "without hurting him," he meant "without damaging him so much he won't be a good bait any more." The "hurt" to be prevented was not pain to the frog but damage to the frog as an effective bait. Note also the interesting folklore about the frog, whose mouth was said to "close up" after August.

But notice also that the goal was to keep the bait animal alive as long as possible even after all this hardware had been introduced into its body. Jim Rose's excellent work on the fish's inability to feel pain does nothing to reduce my certainty that this was fiendish treatment of a living creature.

TORTUR'D WORMS AND LIVING INSECTS

In the long and checkered history of angling-related verse, only a handful of poets have achieved critical success, and most serious students of such verse would say that John Gay was one of the finest—and one of the very few still worth reading today. He is best remembered by anglers, and often anthologized, for some fly-fishing related poems in *Rural Sports* (1713), which included such gracious celebrations of fly fishing and fly tying as this praise of the artisanship of fly tying:

> *To frame the little animal provide*
> *All the gay hues that wait on femal pride,*
> *Let nature guide thee; sometimes golden wire*
> *The shining bellies of the fly require;*
> *The peacock's plumes thy tackle must not fail,*
> *Nor the dear purchase of the sable's tail.*
> *Each gaudy bird some slender tribute brings,*
> *And lends the growing insect proper wings;*
> *Silks of all colours must their aid impart,*
> *And every fur promote the fisher's art.*
> *So the gay lady, with expensive care,*
> *Borrows the pride of land, of sea, and air;*
> *Furs, pearls, and plumes, the glittering thing displays,*
> *Dazles our eyes, and easie hearts betrays.*[21]

British poet John Gay (1685–1732) was among the first writers to proclaim the moral superiority of fly fishing over other forms of angling. His poems claimed this superiority on the grounds that fly fishers did not require bait, and thus did not mistreat worms, insects, small fish, and frogs as did bait fishermen.

ILLUSTRATION BY MARSHA KARLE FROM AN ENGRAVING IN *THE POETICAL WORKS OF JOHN GAY,* VOLUME I, EDITED BY JOHN UNDERHILL (LONDON: LAWRENCE AND BULLEN, 1893).

There are some pleasantly interesting subtleties here, including his reference to "femal pride," presumably an allusion to the use of a wide variety of natural fibers and feathers in human female garments; the reference to the fly as a "gay lady" (a very early ascription of gender to an artificial fly); and the "easie heart" of the fish that is "betrayed" by the artificial fly (a different and apparently less odious kind of betrayal than using a small fish to catch a big fish). Among the early British fly-fishing writers, Gay perhaps most competently moved the discussion of fly-fishing practice into the realm of such metaphors and abstractions.

But Gay also took up the cruelty chorus, and in doing so became one of the first writers to overtly contrast the supposedly inherent badness of bait fishing with the higher moral purity of fly fishing:

> *I never wander where the bord'ring reeds*
> *O'erlook the muddy stream, whose tangling weeds*
> *Perplex the fisher; I, nor chuse to bear*
> *The thievish nightly net, nor barbed spear;*
> *Nor drain I ponds the golden carp to take,*
> *Nor trowle for pike, dispeoplers of the lake.*
> *Around the steel no tortur'd worm shall twine,*
> *No blood of living insect stain my line;*
> *Let me, less cruel, cast the feather'd hook,*
> *With pliant rod athwart the pebbled brook,*
> *Silent along the mazy margin stray,*
> *And with the fur-wrought fly delude the prey.*[22]

Here, Gay, by choosing to fly-fish, left behind the messy, poacher-preferred net and spear. He refused to participate in the crudest of approaches—simply draining the whole pond and picking up the helpless fish.[23] He even discarded trolling, which at that time did not mean dragging a lure behind a boat, but using a long rod (and probably not a reel) to toss a baited hook as far across a water as possible and then dragging it back toward you (for reasons that remain obscure, this form of trolling infuriated some anglers as unsporting).

Most important for our purposes, Gay declared his independence of the cruel techniques that impaled living creatures on hooks. The largest British mayfly species were routinely cast on a light line in the same way as were artificial flies, and of course worms were fished in all the ways worms can still be fished.[24]

No more, said Gay. I'm a fly fisher and I'm above such reprehensible acts.

A variety of social and cultural forces were at work here. One of them that would have so much to do with the future of fly fishing was the common human urge for exclusivity—for feeling a little special, privileged, or superior. Fly fishers latched onto this opportunity quite early, recognizing that their freedom from organic baits did set them up to feel pretty good about themselves. Not only were they not hacking away at small living creatures, they were also not soiling their hands with worm guts and all those stinky and distasteful paste recipes that were the heart and soul of bait fishing.[25] By contrast, as Gay so eloquently described, fly fishers dealt only with beautiful things, especially in the long list of natural materials involved in the tying of their flies.

But a cultured person like Gay would also have felt the currents of romanticism and the changing religious views of the time. As historian Keith Thomas has said, "From the later seventeenth century onwards, it had thus become an acceptable Christian doctrine that all members of God's creation were entitled to civil usage."[26] Out of this mood and time came a clarified notion of what should most concern us in our dealings with, and respect for, our fellow living creatures. The crux of subsequent deliberations on these important matters was solidified in a single statement by the utilitarian philosopher Jeremy Bentham, in 1789: "The question is not, Can they *reason?* nor, Can they *talk?* but, Can they *suffer?*"[27] Pain wasn't just one of the questions to be dealt with in our relationship with other species; it was the central question. With his complete avoidance of live bait and his devotion to the fineries of fly tying, Gay would have felt much elevated from his fellow anglers in responding to that question.

SETTING FLY FISHING APART

I have often complained of the shortage of evidence in fly-fishing history. Especially in the years before 1800, we are dependent upon only a few fishing books and other random items for almost our entire impression of what the anglers of those days thought and how they fished. We simply don't know enough. But if we accept those relatively few published writings as at least suggestive of what was going on at any given time, then Gay's poetry tells us that something very important was happening. It had to do with holding fly fishing separate from and finer than other kinds of fishing.

This was not any absolute or abrupt change. Only a few decades before Gay wrote, Charles Cotton produced one of the great masterpieces of fly-fishing instruction—an extended essay that also quite enthusiastically included competent advice on worm fishing.[28] As important, many of our leading fly-fishing authorities in subsequent centuries—for example the British experts William Stewart and Francis Francis in the nineteenth century and the Americans Ray Bergman and Joe Brooks in the twentieth century—were all-around anglers, eagerly fishing, as Bergman once captured in a book title, "with fly, plug, and bait."

But even admitting the continuation of bait fishing by many outstanding fly anglers, Gay's poetry demonstrated that by the beginning of the seventeenth century there were self-identified *exclusive* fly fishers who distinguished themselves from all other anglers, and also thought themselves superior to the rest. Fly fishing's "airs" as a finer kind of sport can be sensed in some writings even earlier than this, but by Gay's time they had taken on an explicit moral tone. Fly fishing, Gay said and implied, was practiced by better people. They were not just richer, not just more aesthetically sensitive, not just more accomplished. They embraced and exemplified higher moral standards. We've never entirely recovered from this self-elevation.

Gay himself provided us with the first evidence that such snootiness is highly risky. Yes, he was right that in vivid contrast with the smelly, gooey, and otherwise offensive gunk that bait fishers had to lug around, fly fishers did indeed enjoy the beauty of so many wonderful fly-tying materials. But those very materials are just another sign of animal misery—in all the birds and mammals whose lives were cut short, often by cruel traps, frenzied hunting dogs, or aerial nets, so that the delicately sensitized Mr. Gay could rhapsodize at the streamside about the beauty of each feather and fur. That he understood this flaw in his position in some remote way is suggested by his remark about the "dear purchase of the sable's tail."[29]

Though I don't want to succumb to the writing of a separate and very different essay here, Gay's writings also serve to introduce a trend in fly fishing that has over the centuries given the sport a reputation, and at times even a notoriety, as an act that is at the same time both intensively engaged in nature and almost tragically divorced from nature. As nonconsumptive nature-related activities (backpacking, bird-watching, botanizing, canoeing, photography, and so on) have become more and more popular (to the point that they are consumptive just because of the trampling, mobbing, and other collateral damage caused by their hordes of enthusiasts), fly fishers have more and more often found themselves grouped with these nonconsumers.[30]

While many of us praise these activities, and especially fly fishing, for its sensitivity to protecting ecological settings and reducing our effect on those settings, other observers see this as an emasculation of something important and see fly fishing as a ster-

Since at least the 1700s, fly fishers' assertions that they were less cruel because they did not have to kill small animals for bait have seemed somewhat disingenuous considering the many animals that died to provide them with the furs and feathers needed to create their flies. This earliest known illustration of a fly tier at his bench appeared, beginning in 1760, in many printings and variations of John Hawkins' important edition of Walton's *The Compleat Angler*.

ile shadow of its original, traditional purposes. Ironies pile on ironies as fly fishing, now criticized by some for its catch-and-release culture of cruelty, is seen by others as a prissy and sterile version of a traditional field sport, a pastime that has become essentially meaningless as a real sport because it now gets along without, quite literally, any blood and guts.

ATTACKS AND DEFENSES

There is some disagreement among historical scholars over the process by which, and even the extent to which, our attitudes about animals have changed over the past few centuries.[31] It is certainly true that we dare not speak too confidently about the nature of similar changes in angling attitudes since medieval times. Our information base is too small for us to interpret it with certainty.

For example, as I've already suggested, I don't know if either the apparent values of anglers, or the apparent intensification of public disapproval of angling were accurately reflected in the surviving writings of a relatively small body of educated angling enthusiasts and their critics in the eighteenth and nineteenth centuries. Some of these apparent changes may have been caused by more people actively taking one position or another, or perhaps the changes we think we see in the historical record were just artifacts of more people writing and publishing, and thus exposing their opinions to our view. Whatever the case, in the early 1800s, more people had more to say, in print, on the matter of fishing and its moral failings.

The critics certainly were prominent. In 1799, essayist and critic Charles Lamb described anglers as "patient tyrants, meek inflictors of pangs intolerable, [and] cool devils."[32] Even more famously, in 1819 Lord Byron, creator of heroic poetry, exclaimed, "But Anglers! No Angler can be a good man."[33] More insulting, he took on Izaak Walton himself:

> *Angling, too, that solitary vice,*
> *Whatever Izaak Walton sings or says:*
> *The quaint, old, cruel coxcomb, in his gullet*
> *Should have a hook, and a small trout to pull it.*[34]

With this kind of attention, and a variety of social movements relating to the protection and treatment of animals generally, anglers felt the fire more and more. If deliberations on these issues had seemed distant or abstract in previous centuries, they no longer were so easily ignored. Though intermittent and often ineffectual efforts had been made to ban this or that form of cruelty to some species of animal in both England and America since the 1600s, animal welfare was the focus of a variety of movements and legislative acts in the nineteenth century. As more citizens, journalists, and advocates adhered to the view that "England is the hell of dumb animals," society slowly began to adjust.[35]

Starting in 1822, a series of bills and revisions of bills against cruelty to animals were passed by Parliament. The Royal Society for the Prevention of Cruelty to Animals was founded in 1824. Not coincidentally, the Vegetarian Society was established in 1847. As these and many other political and social steps were taken in defense of animals, sportsmen had no choice but to notice.

In fact, I suspect that the attention that sportsmen, especially fly fishers, paid to this swelling public opposition to cruelty might have been greater than that paid by many other people. It is obvi-

Lord Byron (1788–1824) was among the most prominent early-nineteenth-century critics of angling as a cruel sport, once proclaiming that "no angler can be a good man."
ILLUSTRATION BY MARSHA KARLE FROM CONTEMPORARY PORTRAIT REPRODUCED AS PROJECT GUTENBERG ETEXT 13619.JPG.

ous that cruelty of the worst kind to many domestic animals continued, despite increasing social disapproval and legal suppression, through much of the nineteenth century.

But remember that these fly fishers, at least the most self-conscious and status-conscious of them, had probably embraced Gay's view, and had already become quite comfortable thinking of themselves as the finest, brightest, and most enlightened of all anglers. To stand unmoved in the face of accusations of cruelty, especially when at least some of those charges were so telling, wouldn't have made sense to them.

In his book *A True Treatise on the Art of Fly-Fishing* (1838), William Shipley echoed and elaborated on the sentiments so eloquently expressed by John Gay in the previous century:

Fly-fishing is exempt from the principal drawbacks attendant on the other modes of angling. In the first place, the charge of cruelty cannot, with any justice, attach to it. The fly fisher tortures no insect, no reptile, no living animal, in pursuing his recreation. He uses artificial baits; and even the charge, that the fish he kills is put to unnecessary torture, cannot be thoroughly substantiated. Sir Humphrey Davy, a great authority on any point that relates to the organisation of fishes, says, and we entirely agree with him, that "it cannot be doubted, that the nervous system of fish, and cold-blooded animals in general, is less sensitive than that of warm-blooded animals. The hook is usually fixed in the cartilaginous part of the mouth, where there are no nerves; and a proof, that the sufferings of a hooked fish cannot be great, is found in the circumstance, that though a trout has been hooked and played for some minutes, he will often, after his escape with the artificial fly in his mouth, take the natural fly, and feed as if nothing had happened; having apparently learnt only from the experiment, that the artificial-fly is not proper for food. And I have caught pikes with four or five hooks in their mouths, and tackle which they had broken only a few minutes before; and the hooks seem to have had no other effect than that of serving as a sort of *sauce piquante*, urging them to seize another morsel of the same kind.[36]

Invoking the eminent Davy would have made almost any angler of that day feel reinforced, but Davy himself, in *Salmonia* (1828), had already admitted ambivalence on these matters. In fact, Shipley's quote of Davy was somewhat disingenuous, as it left out Davy's opening remark on the subject. Davy did not start with "it cannot be doubted. . . ." He started by saying, "I have already admitted the danger of analysing, too closely, the moral character of any of our field-sports; yet I think it cannot be doubted . . . etc."[37] Our smartest fly-fishing ancestors knew we were on thin ice, and some of them even tried to warn us. As one of the characters in Davy's *Salmonia* put it, "The advocates for a favourite pursuit never want sophisms to defend it. I have even heard it asserted, that a hare enjoys being hunted."[38]

But most of us weren't ready to listen to cautionary wisdoms, or were too distracted by the apparent force of our own arguments. Besides, there's no question that Shipley had some interesting arguments mixed in with his self-righteous bluster. Just as many modern anglers have witnessed some fish behavior that suggests that fish are impervious to the pain of the hook, Shipley offered one of the most vivid, if not lurid, examples of apparent evidence of this sort to be published in the sport's literature. He related this story told by an acquaintance.

The following fact ought to put an end to any doubts we may have relative to the insensibility of fish: "Some time ago, two young gentlemen of Dumfries, while fishing at *Dalswinton Loch*, having expended their stock of worms, &c., had recourse to the expedient of picking out the eyes of the dead perch, and attaching them to their hooks, a bait which the perch is known to take quite as readily as any other. One of the perch caught in this manner struggled so much when taken out of the water, that the hook had been no sooner loosened from its mouth, than

The prominent scientist Humphrey Davy (1778–1829), though an avid angler and the author of the popular *Salmonia; or Days of Fly-Fishing* (1828), recognized the legitimate ethical quandaries faced by sportsmen and warned his fellow anglers about "the danger of analysing, too closely, the moral character of any of our field-sports."

ILLUSTRATION BY MARSHA KARLE FROM A SAMUEL WILLIAM REYNOLDS PORTRAIT
(BASED ON A THOMAS PHILLIPS MEZZOTINT), PUBLISHED IN 1822.

it came in contact with one of its own eyes, and actually tore it. The pain, if so it can be called, occasioned by this accident only made the fish struggle the harder, until at last it fairly slipped through the holder's fingers, and again escaped to its native element. The disappointed fisher, still retaining the eye of the aquatic fugitive, adjusted it on the hook, and again committed his line to the waters. After a very short interval, on pulling up the line, he was astonished to find the identical perch that had eluded his grasp a few minutes before, and which literally perished by *swallowing its own eye!*"[39]

Exactly what such stories proved about the pain-sensing capabilities of fish—or, indeed, their reasoning faculties—remains a good bit less clear than Shipley might have preferred to believe. But as a counter-argument against claims of great cruelty, they certainly would have eased the minds of anglers who wondered about such things and wanted to believe that fish were impervious to pain.[40]

THE MATURING OF SYMPATHY: RAYMOND'S CODE

Anglers could only do so much to ease the hostility of the critics, and could probably do no more to ease their own anxieties about the possible cruelty of their sport. They were, however, becoming more accomplished at defining the limitations of how far they could go in reducing perceived cruelty. In 1866, there appeared a pleasant little fishing manual whose goal was to advise anglers, in all practical terms, on how to keep that cruelty to a minimum: *The Art of Fishing on the Principle of Avoiding Cruelty, with Approved Rules for Fishing Used During Sixty Years' Practice, Not Hitherto Published in Any Work on the Subject*, by Reverend Oliver Raymond.[41]

It was an extraordinary little tract that hasn't deserved the oblivion into which it's fallen. Reverend Raymond displayed a reasonably complete breadth of familiarity with the things that were of concern to fishing's critics, and he addressed them systematically and with sympathy for the fish, the fishermen, and the anti-fishermen.

Raymond gave the following outraged description of the procedure used by one bait fisherman,

> a brute, and worse, with two legs, which is a far milder name than such an operator deserves, who catches a frog, scrapes his back with a knife, and sprinkles him with *aqua fortis*, to make him shriek and cry out, when thus put upon the hook, and thrown on the water, to entice his enemy the pike to come and devour him?
>
> "*Contemplation and action*," says Isaac Walton, "*are combined in the art of angling*." If the above cruel process be the action, what must the contemplation be? Let us hope that no one, save a thoughtless, uncontemplative person, could resort to such a cruel, merciless, and surely we may add fiendish method of pastime.

Raymond provided the first succinct and complete code of behavior for the compassionate angler. He was candid and forthright enough to say that fishing could not be made perfectly painless and merciful. He explained that his book was a "treatise, on the best mode of rendering fishing a merciful pursuit,"[42] the "principal object" of the book was "to reduce the practice to the principle of mercy. We speak here as regards comparative mercy; since field and river sports cannot in themselves be devoid altogether of pain and suffering to those animals or fish we endeavor to capture. I would here, by the way, remark that the river sport is far less cruel than the field sports."[43]

Making fishing as merciful as possible was, according to Raymond, a matter of a few simple rules. For one, if you're going to use bait, capture and kill it promptly:

KILL THE BAIT BEFORE YOU USE IT.

I am now entering on the merciful mode of angling; and to draw particular attention to this part of the work, I give the first merciful direction in capital letters. "Yes—but, ah!" says one, "there is nothing like a *live bait*." This I deny, and would not fear, were I in the habit of betting, to risk a considerable sum of money that I would with a snap hook, properly baited with a *dead* gudgeon, we will say, or any other small fish, equal, if not surpass the success of the merciless angler who impales when alive the poor defenceless little bait, and keeps him writhing on the hook, to entice the ravenous pike, or passes a wire down his back, and thus spits him alive, that he may the longer live on his hook.[44]

For another, use no other kind of live bait—no worm, no mayfly, nothing that can suffer on the hook.

For another, use blunt rather than sharp hooks so that you do the least harm and cause the least pain to the fish. Just as modern barbless-hook fishermen maintain that if you keep a tight line you will land as many fish on barbless hooks as on barbed hooks, Raymond insisted that he could land as many fish on dull hooks as on sharp ones.

For another, land fish carefully. In discussed trolling for pike, he said, "never land him, whether he be small or great, without a landing net, or taking him carefully out of the water with your hands—but not by putting your fingers in his eyes, a method recommended by some barbarous anglers."[45]

For another, kill any fish the instant you land it. "Death, it is true, is the fate of the captured fish, but not a *lingering death*, unless unnecessarily made so by the merciless fisherman."[46]

For another, there is no need to use natural flies, because a competent artificial fly fisher can outfish the natural fly fisher anyway. This was a matter of some dispute, and many anglers would have argued otherwise, just as many bait fishers (and fly fishers) today still assume that bait will catch more fish. What is most interesting in Raymond's condemnation of fishing with natural flies is his passionate defense of the "right" of those flies to have their own lives. In this, we find Raymond empathizing with another species of animal in the strongest terms yet used among angling writers:

> Away then with the *live* fly, and leave him to enjoy his existence in the sunny ray. One day's existence is frequently his utmost limit: let him enjoy his short-lived nature, and cut him not off in the meridian sunshine of his day; open your drake basket and let him escape; and as he enjoys his liberty, ascending with majestic motion in the glorious sunlight, your relenting heart will experience an inward joy as you view his heavenward flight far greater than having made him the victim of your cruelty for securing your prey.[47]

"The recollection of your mercy," Raymond concluded, "in avoiding, by every possible care, to inflict pain on your captured victims, will give a zest to your anticipation of another day's fishing, with its general accompaniments of balmy air, refreshing breeze, to contemplate the works of God, in Nature's lovely scenes, beside the bubbling current or tranquil stream."[48]

I have so far only mentioned religion in passing, but the good reverend here captures the tangled essence of the Western approach to sport. We want to revel in God's wonders along the stream, but as the historian Lynn White once put it, Christianity is "the most anthropocentric religion the world has seen."[49] Our idea of how best to honor those wonders is, by the standards of human cultures generally, exceptionally dominating. In many ways, we seek to re-engineer and redesign that setting to suit our tastes, just as some of us, like Reverend Raymond, may justify our sporting code in terms of religious convictions. Some of us invoke our Christian beliefs to justify our treatment of other animals, while others invoke our Christian beliefs to condemn those same treatments and advocate others.[50] Like cruelty and sport itself, God's word is always open to interpretation and debate.

COMPARATIVE MERCY

We could comfortably end this historical tour of the development of fly fishing's self-image as the least cruel type of angling with Raymond's book—not because fishing stopped changing then, but because his code of behavior, combined with the literary exhortations and prescriptions of Gay, Shipley, and Davy, encapsulate most of the modern fly fisher's view of himself and his sport in these matters of alleged or necessary cruelty. We had the larger arguments in our defense pretty well constructed by the late 1800s. We may have polished up some of these arguments since then, and some of our attempts to do so have indeed refined the substance of our case, but if you ask Joe Flyfisher about pain in fish, you're still most likely going to hear some variant on the Gay/Shipley/Davy/Raymond theme.

We should know, however, that in recent decades academics from a variety of disciplines have taken on the same topics and dug much deeper into the questions involved in the cruelty debate, to the point where there is now a thriving formal literature not only on fish pain and stress but on the complex ethical questions anglers face when hooking, playing, and landing fish. We can only hope that the substance of this stimulating and intellectually demanding literature will begin to seep out into the larger public arena, the way that Jim Rose's work on fish pain already has. And indeed, Rose himself is one of the contributors to the rigorous new scholarly conversation on our relationship to fish. Interested readers could beneficially begin an exploration of this material by reading his paper, "Anthropomorphism and 'mental welfare' of fishes," in the May 4, 2007, *Diseases of Aquatic Organisms*.

Until we do take on the chore of this more demanding reading, I assume that most of us will continue to echo the arguments and stances—the strong ones and the weak ones—established by the time Raymond published his little book.[51] It was about that time, in fact, that fly fishers seemed to find other things to worry about and the cruelty issue—perhaps because it seemed to have been sorted out about as well as it could—came up a lot less often, proportionately at least, in our published conversations.

Among other things, we fly fishers were still very busy right then firming up our own sense of specialness. In the closing decades of the nineteenth century, under the impetus of the "dry-fly revolution" (angling historian Tony Hayter's term for the rigid approach to fly fishing so successfully promoted by Frederic Halford and his followers in the late 1800s), many fly fishers became ever more exclusive in their practice. They defined themselves not as anglers but as fly fishers. And in this society of fly fishers, we became more and more divided into competing and even opposing schools of thought and practice. It is safe to say that in any generation of fly fishers since Halford's first book was published in 1886 we have spent far more time criticizing each other's ideas about the proper practice of fly fishing than we have spent wondering about the possible cruelty of the sport. Any of us who worried at all about cruelty probably reasoned that we were at the top of the scale in Raymond's measurement of "comparative mercy" and could do little, short of stopping fishing altogether, to become even more merciful.[52]

Which adds yet another irony to this story. As I explained at the beginning of this chapter, in the closing decades of the twentieth century, after a long life as a minor regulation in a few special locations, catch-and-release fishing became a widespread management tool, angling philosophy, and (some would say) quasi-religious belief. And while it was accurately heralded as a key to conservation and progressive fisheries management, the popularization of catch-and-release fishing at the same time plunged the great-great-grandchildren of Reverend Raymond's righteous fly fishers down to the very bottom of the "comparative mercy" scale. If an angler could be faulted for fishing with "treacherous" tortured baits, or allowing captured fish to die a slow death, or in other ways causing the death of his fish to be unnecessarily difficult and painful, how much worse was an angler who put the fish through all that and then, with seeming callous disrespect and thoughtless cruelty, turned the fish loose so that another angler, or the same angler, could put it through the same mistreatment again?

Here we must come back to a lapse of attention to an important detail in our present excitement and self-satisfaction over Dr. Rose's important publication on the inability of fish to feel pain. Our critics tell us that even if we do not cause the fish pain, we are still being cruel to them. Compassion is not just about how to avoid inflicting physical agony.

NOT OFF THE HOOK

Like many other fishermen who have thought in even undisciplined ways about the fish we hook, I have had doubts about the pain the fish was supposedly feeling. I reasoned through it like this. The typical, casual critics of fishing (who in their own way are as anthropocentric as the rest of us) seemed to assume that the hook caused the fish pain just as it would hurt a human who was similarly hooked. But if a human were hooked in the mouth, the last thing such a person would do is strain against the hook, much less run like hell on a tight line or jump wildly in the air. Such behavior would only intensify the pain and increase the damage. Thinking about it this way, I figured that if I were hooked, I would do all I could to minimize the pain, even if that meant moving directly toward the person who hooked me to ensure a slack line (and for other more vengeful reasons, of course).

Thus I guessed—"assumed" would be too strong a word—that the fish must be struggling for other reasons than physical pain. I also figured that the most important of those reasons must have to do with the restriction of its freedom.

We can't assume, however, that the fish understands that being hooked means it will be captured and killed. Perhaps if it's been caught and released a few times, it knows the drill, and in that case perhaps it will fight to prevent being captured again.

It has also been theorized, however, that fish caught and released many times may fight less because they *do* know that the sooner they are landed, the sooner they will be released. Exactly why the fish struggles against the hook and line is probably a complicated combination of impulses, most of which have to do with the fish's evolutionary engineering to survive. The incredible and even life-threatening expenditure of energy that the fish puts into its efforts to escape indicates that, whatever its reasons for struggling, something in its nervous system has defined the stakes as very high. Whether or not the fish "knows" that it is fighting for its life (or even knows that it *has* a life), it is functionally doing just that.

Just by establishing that fish can't experience pain the way we do, or even by establishing that they can't experience terror, or fear, or anxiety in the way we humans understand those emotions, we are not exempting ourselves from some heavy responsibilities in the enterprise of going out there and hooking them.

We have often wondered what to call this process by which we land a fish. When we talk about hooking a fish, we make much of the "fight" of the fish. But what kind of a "fight" is it? It is often argued that, with the exception of a few really huge species of sport fish, ones that could actually do us grave harm, we are "playing," rather than "fighting" the fish we catch. At least for us, it's more "play" than "fight." Given the odds of our past experience, each fish has a very high likelihood of being landed, while for us losing the "fight" means only that the fish escaped. There is not the exchange of meaningfully reciprocal violence that might justify the term "fight."[53]

The "playing" or "fighting" of hooked fish has come under increased scrutiny in modern times, both among anglers who are concerned with the survival of exhausted fish and among critics troubled by the perceived cruelty of the process. But the excitement of landing a big fish is an enduring element of the fishing experience, as shown by this somewhat overdramatized 1884 illustration from a fishing-tackle advertisement showing an angler apparently preparing to gaff a fish in a waterfall.
COURTESY OF THE AMERICAN MUSEUM OF FLY FISHING, MANCHESTER, VT.

John McPhee, on the other hand, is incensed at the term "playing," which he feels is just a euphemism for "at best torturing and at worst killing a creature you may or may not eat."[54] But McPhee, by his angry attack on the whole catch-and-release philosophy, has perhaps disqualified himself from participation in this terminological quandary. He already admitted that he hates the whole business, so why should we trust his opinion on its subtleties?

I recently mentioned this awkward terminology to fly-fishing historian and commentator Ken Cameron, wondering if there was a better term for that stage of the process following the hookup and preceding the capture:

> Well, I doubt that fishermen want to give up "play" and "fight," which sound so artistic and manly. But a sociologist/biologist might talk about "panic behavior" or some such. I can just see fishing articles in which we said, "The fish gave me a great panic behavior, and his in-close desperation was terrific." Or, we could borrow a page from Lenny Bruce and use "blah-blah." "The fish gave me a terrific blah-blah, and when I got him to the boat he really blah-blah'd. I've never seen such a blah-blah in a fish."[55]

Which is to say, I think, that we're stuck with inadequate words here. Sorry, John; I don't think even *The New Yorker*'s legendary fact-checkers and word-crafters can edit us out of this one.

So what are we to make of the fish's struggle to escape from our hook? Even if the fish has no notion of its own life and potential death, and even if it is not trying to escape from pain or fear, and even if its "fight" is the result of some hard-wiring that has nothing to do with either physiological discomfort or emotional feelings, it is still struggling as hard as it can. We are responsible for that struggle.

It is and should be of considerable comfort to us that modern science has demonstrated that a hooked fish is not capable of feel-

Anglers' portrayals of themselves have often inspired criticism from skeptics who doubt the value of outdoor sports. William Henry Harrison Murray's 1869 book *Adventures in the Wilderness* (see chapter two for more on Murray) celebrated the fishing experience in such unrealistic terms that even other anglers objected. His illustration of a trout jumping about five feet into the air—and seeming about to attack the angler—was lampooned in the sporting press as an unseemly exaggeration even for a fisherman.

ing the sort of pain, fear, or rage we would expect (and be outraged by) in a similarly hooked bird, deer, or squirrel. It certainly is a relief to me. But we're still doing what we're doing. We're still hooking a living animal and jerking it around pretty thoroughly, at great risk to its life even if we intend to release it. Our sport may not depend upon the fish suffering physical pain. It may not depend upon the fish suffering terror or fear. But it does require us to stress the fish in other ways that, even if they don't hurt, place upon us an accountability we have not yet fully considered.

As in the past several centuries of deliberations over the ethical quandaries of angling, this isn't really about the fish. It's about us.

Just as those critics of angling several centuries ago were primarily concerned with the moral compromises we might be making by our "deceitful" use of bait, or by our culpability in bringing out the rapacious tendency in a fish by providing it the opportunity to eat a smaller fish, we are called upon, by our society if not by our consciences, to consider the deeper personal consequences of what we're doing.

As I watch this play out today, I see some anglers quit fishing altogether because they decide not only that there is a moral price in this process of hooking fish, but also that the moral price is just too high.

I see other anglers incorporate a heightened awareness of that moral price into their sense of what matters about going fishing. Rather than perceiving or experiencing the struggle of the fish as a cheap thrill (as they are so often accused of doing), these anglers at least strive to connect with the fish's struggle for survival on much more profound levels—and to do so with commensurate gratitude for the opportunity and soul-searching awareness of the moral complexities of the moment.[56]

I see other anglers shake their heads at the apparent irresolvability of the issues and just go back to fishing because it feels like the right thing to do. Eventually, coming to terms with many of our most perplexing dilemmas is just that—coming to terms with them rather than solving them, even if the terms we settle upon don't involve any clearly stated personal rule or code.[57] We just get on with it.

And of course mostly I see anglers not bothering to pay any attention to these questions at all; either because they don't care, they don't know about them, they don't want to know about them, they don't have any doubt about the rightness of what they're doing when they fish, or for other reasons of their own. To their credit, these unthinking folks do provide a massive social inertia that keeps us from going off the deep end every time a new idea comes down the pike. They're pretty much immune to ideas.

Seeing all these people, and hearing their often eloquently made cases for this or that perspective on the ethical issues we've struggled with the past few centuries when we hook fish, I also see myself here and there among them, taking this or that view, on any given day, on any given cast, with any given fish.

SCREAM

For all participants in the debates, dialogues, and rants over the cruelty of fishing, eloquence is a treacherous friend. Eloquence infuriates the inarticulate because they find themselves seemingly out-argued by someone who may just be a more able arguer. Eloquence seduces the sympathetic who might be well advised not to go along with an argument just because it sounds so good and gives such comfort. But a point powerfully made is usually worth hearing, so in this matter of pain-giving anglers and pain-receiving fish, let's close this chapter, and this book, with two opposing, complicated, and equally sturdy views.

Odell Shepard's *Thy Rod and Thy Creel* (1930), though little known among anglers, is one of the wisest and most gracious of fishing books. Shepard, a scholar, poet, and Pulitzer Prize–winning biographer, described catching a beautiful trout while fishing for bass and pike.

Altogether, he looked like an unusually gorgeous little sunrise as he lay there on the gunwale of my boat, making no strenuous effort to escape but merely opening and closing his mouth in well-bred protest. I looked at him; I enlarged my former conception of the splendors that the world contains; then I unhooked him very gently and put him back into the water. It would have been an indignity to dump him into my basket with a mess of scoundrelly bass and pickerel; and as for preparing him for supper, I should almost as soon have cooked a baby angel.[58]

The British critic, essayist, and journalist Leigh Hunt, writing in the early 1800s, told a story that, though its origin seems lost to modern commentators, has worked its way into angling lore, a cautionary tale that captures the dilemma we modern anglers face. In this fable-like vignette, a college dean encountered a young man fishing, and asked him if he had ever caught a fish called the Scream. "The man protested that he had never heard of such a fish. 'What!' says the Dean, 'you an angler, and never heard of the fish that gives a shriek when coming out of the water? 'Tis the only fish that has a voice, and a sad, dismal sound it is.' The man asked who could be so barbarous as to angle for a creature that shrieked. 'That,' said the Dean, 'is another matter; but what do you think of fellows that I have seen, whose only reason for hooking and tearing all the fish they can get at, is that they do *not* scream?"[59]

Despite its beautifully stated admission that the sight of a single trout could enlarge one's conception of the splendors that the world contains, and its amazing allusion to the baby angel, Shepard's statement is mostly forgotten. But Hunt's little tale, or at least its core message, has made its winding way down the generations and become a part of fishing's own folk wisdom. If you hear it today, it will most likely be from a fellow angler. And it is usually reduced to the one sentence that suggests that whether or not fish feel pain, and whether or not they feel fear, we still have a lot to think about when we set the hook in one. It goes like this: "If fish could scream, a lot of things would be different."[60]

ACKNOWLEDGMENTS

As always, I must thank my spouse Marsha Karle first, for her enthusiasm and support and for being such wonderful company on all our travels along America's historic waters. And this time I also thank her for the fun portraits of historic angling characters that illustrate this book.

For about thirty years now I have enjoyed an informative and vastly entertaining correspondence with my friend Ken Cameron, novelist and historian, about everything to do with fly fishing and its quirky history. Dedicating a book to him seems an insufficient note of appreciation to someone who has written so thoughtfully and provocatively about this great sport.

This book is only possible because about six years ago, over a nice lunch at the Mammoth Hot Springs Hotel in Yellowstone, Phil Monahan invited me to contribute a column on angling history to *American Angler*. Almost all the chapters in this book began life in those columns. This work has given me the delightful opportunity to explore more deeply many topics only lightly dealt with in my books *American Fly Fishing: A History* (1987), and *Royal Coachman* (1998). My thanks to Phil for sticking with this peculiar historical enterprise all this time. Very short forms of Chapters 1, 2,

3, 4, 5, and 7 first appeared in *American Angler*. Chapter 6, "Outworn Privileges," is a considerably rewritten and expanded rendition of a conference paper that first appeared as "Yellowstone Fishing and Fisheries Management: A Continuing Experiment," pages 9–13 in M. Hagengruber and B. Wiltshire, eds., *Fish, Fishing and Fisheries Management in Yellowstone National Park, An Educational Conference*, published by the Federation of Fly Fishers, Bozeman, Montana, 1998. I think of this chapter as an advancement on topics that John Varley and I discussed in our book *Yellowstone Fishes*, originally published as *Freshwater Wilderness* in 1983 and expanded and republished by Stackpole Books in 1999, and that I also discussed in my book *Mountain Time* (1984).

Rick Balkin, my agent and friend for more than twenty years now, saw the book through its acceptance by my friends at Stackpole Books, where Judith Schnell, Amy Lerner, and the rest of their team attended to the book with their customary professionalism.

Most of the acknowledging I must do for a book like this is handled in the endnotes, where I try to recognize all the significant sources of information and ideas that are gathered here. But there are many other people I would like to thank.

At the American Museum of Fly Fishing, Gary Tanner, Bill Bullock, Yoshi Akiyama, and Kathleen Achor were unfailingly helpful. Following their initial appearance as columns in *American Angler*, Kathleen has published some of these chapters in their full versions in that institution's splendid journal, *The American Fly Fisher*. As soon as you finish reading this, you should find out how to join the museum; it's doing fly fishers a world of good and far too many of them don't even know it's there.

At Montana State University, philosopher Gordon Brittan has helped more than he knows, both by reminding me of huge areas of scholarship I had bumbled right past, and by inviting me to try out quite a few of the ideas expressed in this book in front of his environmental ethics classes. Former Dean of Libraries Bruce Morton, Special Collections Librarian Kim Scott, and their staff have helped not only by running such an exemplary and exciting research facility but by their devotion to the university's outstanding trout and salmonid collection, which deserves the generous support of thinking anglers everywhere.

At Yellowstone National Park, Park Historian Lee Whittlesey has helped with countless references and lunch conversations about everything to do with the history of the park and cultural and natural resource management. At Yellowstone National Park for many years and now at the Big Sky Institute, John Varley has been perhaps my foremost advisor on the subtleties of natural resource management.

At York University, Toronto, Ontario, historian Richard Hoffmann has helped by his friendship, good counsel, and stellar example of how historical thinking should be practiced.

Others who have helped over the years—by sending me exciting material, doubting my opinions and interpretations, offering their own insights on many subjects, or otherwise helping me keep these inquiries going—include Adrian Bantjes, Bob Barbee, Bob Behnke, Jan Brunvand, David Detweiler, Mike Finley, Bill Eyre, Mary Ann Franke, Gardner Grant, Dale Greenley, Andrew Herd, Wes Hill, Ron Jones, Richard Kress, David Ledlie, the late Starker Leopold, Bud Lilly, Esther Lilly, Leon Martuch, John Merwin, Susan Rhoades Neel, Tom Olliff, Ken Owens, Dave Perkins, Leigh Perkins, Perk Perkins, Datus Proper, John Randolph, James Rose, Tom Rosenbauer, Dianne Russell, Steve Schullery, the late John Townsley, Clark Whitehorn, and Bob Wiltshire.

NOTES

INTRODUCTION: STAND FACING THE RIVER

1. I try not to be too narrow about this. I admit that many other human pursuits arouse similarly intense passions in their practitioners. I've tried more than my share of these endeavors and have the receipts to prove it. But none work so well for me as fly fishing.
2. Roderick Haig-Brown, *A River Never Sleeps* (New York: Crown, 1974), 352.
3. Adrian Franklin, *Animals and Modern Cultures: A Sociology of Human-Animal Relations in Modernity* (London: Sage Publications, 1999), 9, provides a nice example of this phrase as applied to human-animal relationships. This is probably where I first became aware of the phrase as a literary device.
4. Daniel Herman, *Hunting and the American Imagination* (Washington, D.C.: Smithsonian Institution Press, 2001).
5. I talk about the evolution of sport, and about related topics to do with how sport works, in a number of my books, including the overt "histories" I have written, such as *American Fly Fishing: A History* (New York: Nick Lyons Books, 1987) and *The Bear-Hunter's Century: Profiles from the Golden Age of Bear Hunting* (New York: Dodd, Mead and Company, 1988).

CHAPTER ONE: UNCLES AND OTHER HEROES

1. There is a darker side to the expert's achievement, which comes when the expert, as the saying goes, begins to believe his own advertising. Odell Shepard, *Thy Rod and Thy Creel* (New York: Nick Lyons Books, 1984; reprint of 1930 Edwin Valentine Mitchell edition), 38, admitted that "it would be pleasant to have their knowledge and skill, of course, but one would not like to know that one had it. To my thinking there is something even vulgar in such self-confidence, and it seems to me almost as ugly in an angler as it would be in a lover. The man who is absolutely certain that he can catch trout under any and all conditions has no longer any good reason that I can see for doing so."

2. Joseph Campbell, *The Hero with a Thousand Faces* (Princeton, NJ: Princeton University Press, 1949), 37. Invoking Campbell here may not endear me to mainstream anthropologists, in good part because he was such an incurable popularizer; his pronouncements and generalizations often make me nervous, too. But I can't deny his influence on popular notions of culture, and in this case I think quoting him is fair and easily justified.

3. The experiential side of the literature of fishing is filled with—indeed, almost founded upon—quest tales involving some "impossible" fish. They figure prominently in the storytelling genre, as in William Humphrey's big-trout story, *My Moby Dick* (London: Chatto & Windus, 1979), which opens with Humphrey's wonderful bow to Melville's masterpiece, "Call me Bill," or Charles Fox's instructional discussion, in *This Wonderful World of Trout* (Rockville Centre, New York: Freshet Press, 1971), 82–83, of a fish so uncatchable that the local fly fishers had named it "the trout without a mouth"—until Ernest Schwiebert came along and caught it. I used the same device, of a near-mythic trout that cannot be landed, in *Shupton's Fancy: A Tale of the Fly-Fishing Obsession* (Mechanicsburg, PA: Stackpole Books, 1996), which features both the uncatchable fish and the quest for the perfect fly. I suspect that the quest story is not so much a literary device as the sport's defining motif.

4. Thomas Barker, *Barker's Delight: Or, The Art of Angling*, second edition (London: Humphrey Mosely, 1659), 49–50.

5. Charles Cotton, in Izaak Walton, *The Compleat Angler* (London: John Lane, The Bodley Head, 1897; reprint, London: Senate, 1994), 306.

6. Paul Schullery, *American Fly Fishing: A History* (New York: Nick Lyons Books, 1987), 25–31. The best short summary of Porter's career from a fly-fishing point of view is David B. Ledlie, "William T. Porter, First of Our Sporting Journalists," *The American Fly Fisher* 1(3), 1974, 2–4. See also David B. Ledlie, "William T. Porter and the Origins of Imitation," *The American Fly Fisher* 6(2), 1979, 4.

7. Francis Brinley, *The Life of William T. Porter* (New York: D. Appleton, 1860; reprint New York: Arno, 1970), 266. Brinley's book, though adulatory, is a primary biographical source on Porter, and a uniquely valuable reference on sporting attitudes, society, and journalism in his day.

8. For a thorough overview of this period and its sporting journalism see John Reiger, *American Sportsmen and the Origins of Conservation*, third revised edition (Corvallis, OR: Oregon State University Press, 2001).

9. Aldo Leopold, *A Sand County Almanac, and Sketches Here and There* (New York: Oxford University Press, 1949), 181.

10. Gingrich's entertaining, personable, and well-informed books, including *The Well-Tempered Angler* (New York: Alfred Knopf, 1965); *The Joys of Trout* (New York: Crown, 1973); and *The Fishing in Print* (New York: Winchester Press, 1974), were in good part devoted to celebrations of fly fishing's experts. Gingrich did as much as anyone else to establish fly-fishing authorities as celebrities.

CHAPTER TWO: ALL THE LONG-DESIRED THINGS

1. C., "Trout Fishing in Vermont," *American Turf Register and Sporting Magazine*, 1(9), October 1829, 100.

2. Fly-fishing readers will find a nice summary of the history of railroads as they approached the Catskills in Austin Francis, *Catskill Rivers* (New York: Nick Lyons Books, 1983), 22–26.

3. William Henry Harrison Murray, *Adventures in the Wilderness* (Syracuse, NY: Syracuse University Press, 1989). I especially recommend this edition for its helpful foreword by William K. Verner, and its essential introduction by Warder Cadbury. Much of the context in this discussion of mine is based on these sources, as well as Murray's original book and the broader Adirondack historical research I did for Paul Schullery, "'A Sportsman's Paradise,' Fishing and Hunting on the Preserve," in E. Comstock, ed., *The Adirondack League Club 1890–1990* (Old Forge, NY: Adirondack League Club, 1990), 112–61.

4. William C. Stewart, *The Practical Angler* (Edinburgh: Adam and Charles Black, 1857), 6.

5. Andrew Herd, *The Fly* (Ellesmere, Shropshire: The Medlar Press, 2003), 260–61.

6. David Webster, *The Angler and the Loop-Rod* (Edinburgh: William Blackwood and Sons, 1885), 3.

7. Robert Barnwell Roosevelt, *Game Fish of the Northern States of America and British Provinces* (New York: Carleton, 1862), 36–37.

8. John Merwin, *The Battenkill* (New York: Lyons & Burford, 1993), 109.

9. I have provided a general historical overview of the exploration of American waters (at least in the U.S.) by fly fishers in the mid- to late nineteenth century in *American Fly Fishing: A History*, 43–57.

10. Emerson Hough, "Chicago and the West," *Forest and Stream*, January 23, 1890, 7. Emerson Hough is among the American outdoor writers in need of further study. A novelist, conservation writer, and avid sportsman, he informed and entertained generations of readers in the late 1800s and early 1900s. Among his other distinctions, his series of articles in *Forest and Stream* in 1894, on the threats to Yellowstone National Park's last remaining wild bison, led directly to the passage of the first "Lacey Act" protecting park wildlife.

11. Viscount Grey of Fallodon, *Fly Fishing* (London: André Deutsch Limited, 1984 reprint of 1930 edition), 36. I thank Ken Cameron for alerting me to this perfect quotation. Ken's article, "The Dry Fly and Fast Trains," *The American Fly Fisher* 10(1), 2–8, is one of the most important considerations of the changes in angling society brought on by railroad travel. I should mention that though in this discussion I have succumbed to convention and refer to this author as Viscount Grey of Falloden, he was not a lord when his book was first published. He became Viscount Grey in 1916.

12. Paul Schullery, *Mountain Time* (New York: Nick Lyons Books, 1984), 19–30; Paul Schullery, *Royal Coachman: The Lore and Legends of Fly Fishing* (New York: Simon & Schuster, 1999), 157–65.

CHAPTER THREE: SPINNERS AND SINNERS

1. Izaak Walton, *The Compleat Angler* (London: John Lane, 1897; reprint London: Senate, 1994), 106–7.

2. Hewett Wheatley, *The Rod and Line: Or, Practical Hints and Dainty Devices for the Sure Taking of Trout, Grayling, Etc.* (London: Longman, Brown, Green & Longmans, 1849; reprint Mortonehampstead, Devon: The Flyfisher's Classic Library, 2002), 19–42.

3. William Stewart, *The Practical Angler* (Edinburgh: Adam and Charles Black, 1857), 159.

4. J. W. Martin, *My Fishing Days and Ways* (Ellesmere, Shropshire, UK: The Medlar Press, 2004 edition of 1906 original edition), 129, may have described the peak in swivel employment when he wrote that while pike fishing, "I have seen some anglers spinning with a trace that was at least 2 yards long, with four or five swivels at intervals all down its length, under the impression that this quantity of swivels above the lead would prevent any possibility of the line kinking; but I always found that too many swivels defeated the angler's object, and caused a kinking rather than preventing it."

5. Charles Fox, *This Wonderful World of Trout* (Rockville Center, NY: Freshet Press, 1971), 111. There is a photograph of the fish on page 107.

6. Sources on the early years of spin fishing in America include G. Vitt, "Spinning," in A. J. McClane, ed., *The Wise Fisherman's Encyclopedia* (New York: Wm. H. Wise, Inc., 1957), 1096–99; Ira Gabrielson, ed., *The Fisherman's Encyclopedia* (Harrisburg, PA: Stackpole & Heck, 1950), 179–80; and Charles Waterman, *A History of Angling* (Tulsa, OK: Winchester Press, 1981), 221–25.

7. Joseph D. Bates, *Spinning for American Game Fish* (Boston: Little Brown & Company, 1950); A. J. McClane, *Spinning for Fresh and Salt Water Fish of North America* (Englewood Cliffs, NJ: Prentice Hall, 1952). Joe Bates actually wrote four books on spinning in the 1950s, making him the sport's foremost writer-advocate.

8. Paul Schullery, *The Orvis Story: 150 Years of an American Sporting Tradition* (Manchester, VT: The Orvis Company, 2006), 49.

9. Waterman, *A History of Angling*, 224.

10. Waterman, *A History of Angling*, 224.

11. I discuss Hewitt's views on spinning, and quote him at greater length, in *American Fly Fishing: A History*, 190.

12. I discuss this era in fly-fishing writing, when the sport seemed doomed to be eclipsed or replaced by spinning, in *American Fly Fishing: A History*, 190–201. But an excellent recent consideration of this period, especially as it involved Art Flick, is Tom Rosenbauer, "Pioneers & Legends, Art Flick: Everyman's Entomologist," *Eastern Fly Fishing* 1(3), Fall 2005, 28–31. I don't think I've read any other profile of Flick that does as much justice to his gifts, his fly-tying and fly development, and where he fits in the context of his times.

13. Robert Traver, *Trout Madness* (New York: St. Martin's Press, 1960), 39.

14. Ibid., 41.

15. My comments on the early political relationship between the Federation of Fly Fishers and Trout Unlimited in this discussion are based on Arnold Gingrich, *The Joys of Trout* (New York: Crown Publishers, 1973), 115–20, 212–16; my own experiences as a member of Trout Unlimited (and a long-ago officer in the Battenkill Chapter of T.U.) and as a member, senior advisor, and vice president for communications of the Federation of Fly Fishers in the late 1970s and 1980s (when it was still the Federation of Fly Fishermen); and many conversations with several people involved in the leadership of both organizations. I especially thank Bud Lilly, founding president of Montana Trout Unlimited and long-time activist with both organizations, and Esther Lilly, likewise an activist and former official with both organizations.

16. Gingrich, *The Joys of Trout*, 119.

17. Gingrich, *The Joys of Trout*, 120.

18. Russell Chatham, *The Angler's Coast* (New York: Doubleday, 1976), 67.

CHAPTER FOUR:
A GREAT WANT OF TRUE ANGLING SENTIMENT

1. Roderick Haig-Brown, *Fisherman's Spring* (New York: Morrow, 1951), 118–19. As recently as Haig-Brown wrote, he wasn't recent enough to loosen the one-gender grip that dominated writing about outdoor sport for several centuries. For him, it was still all about men.

2. See also my discussion of the distinction between sports and games in *Cowboy Trout* (Helena: Montana Historical Society, 2006), 51–55.

3. John Wilson, "A Case for Competitions," *Fly Fisherman*, February 2004, 22.

4. Izaak Walton, *The Compleat Angler* (London: John Lane, 1897), 223.

5. William Stewart, *The Practical Angler* (Edinburgh: Adam and Charles Black, 1857), 7–8.

6. Charles Chenevix Trench, *A History of Angling* (Chicago: Follett Publishing Company, 1974), 227–28.

7. Cliff Netherton, *History of the Sport of Casting, People, Events, Records, Tackle and Literature, Early Times* (Lakeland, FL: American Casting Educational Association, 1981), 7.

8. John Betts, "Fly Lines and Lineage," *The American Fly Fisher* 26(4), Fall 2000, 18. See also Paul Schullery, "Distance Matters," *American Angler* 30(3), April 2007, 24–25, for more on the development of fly-fishing distance-casting methods.

9. I discussed the distinction between these two kinds of writing in "Occasions for Hope in the Hook and Bullet Press," in *Royal Coachman* (New York: Simon & Schuster, 1999), 172–85.

10. N. W. Simmonds, *Early Scottish Angling Literature* (Shrewsbury, UK: Swan Hill Press, 1997), 33.

11. Andrew Lang, *Angling Sketches* (London: Longmans, Green, and Company, 1891), 81–82.

12. Theodore Gordon, *The Complete Fly Fisherman*, ed. John McDonald (New York: Charles Scribner's, 1947), 229–30.
13. Ted Leeson, *The Habit of Rivers* (New York: The Lyons Press, 1994), 34.
14. Lawrence Sterne, *The Life and Opinions of Tristram Shandy* (London: Ingram, Cooke, and Company, 1853), 43.

CHAPTER FIVE: IF THE FISHES WILL BE PATIENT

1. Henry David Thoreau, *The Portable Thoreau*, ed. Carl Bode (New York: Penguin, 1977), 156.
2. Joshua Gross Rich, "The Trout of Maine Waters—The Rangeley Lakes Region," *American Angler*, April 18, 1883, as quoted in Herbert Shirrefs, *The Richardson Lakes: Jewels in the Rangeley Region* (Bethel, ME: Bethel Historical Society, 1995), 412–13. Nick Karas, *Brook Trout* (New York: The Lyons Press, 1997) quotes another account of Rich's story in which the episode took place in 1854. But the *American Angler* account begins by saying "We will now go back forty years and take a look at these trout before any obstructions were put in, in the shape of dams, and when they have free course to all these waters." According to Shirrefs, *The Richardson Lakes*, 363, Upper Dam, between what are now known as Upper and Lower Richardson Lakes, was first built in 1853, so the two accounts appear to be inconsistent in this minor way. Another helpful account of early Rangeley trout is Austin Hogan, "The Greatest American Brook Trout," *The American Fly Fisher* 1(2), Spring 1974, 6–9. Both Shirrefs and Karas rely heavily on Hogan's summary.
3. Hogan, "The Greatest American Brook Trouts," 9, summarizes a number of reports of the largest fish.
4. Edward Seymour, "Trout-Fishing in the Rangeley Lakes," *Scribner's Monthly* 13(4), February 1877, 9. This is one of the most famous and oft-cited articles written during the time of the Rangeley Lakes excitement, and no doubt contributed to it. A shorter version appeared in Alfred Mayer, ed., *Sport with Gun and Rod in American Woods and Waters* (New York: The Century Company, 1883), 351–78. Both describe the key period in the 1860s when arguments raged, despite the distinguished Professor Agassiz's announcement, over what these fish really were—an argument that probably just further heightened interest in fishing the region.
5. Shirrefs, *The Richardson Lakes*, 363–67, points out that reported dates of construction for *Upper Dam* vary between these years.
6. Hogan, "The Greatest American Brook Trouts," 8, provided this excerpt from an incompletely cited article in *American Sportsman*, 1(1), November, 1872. Hogan, 9, also provided an entertaining episode from 1888, when a man named T. B. Stewart was said to have taken a "double" on brook trout in the pool below Upper Dam, each fish weighing eight pounds. Hogan noted, however, that "some time later in 1888, this same T. B. Stewart was arrested for snagging trout with a grappling hook. He paid his fine, then loudly protested, but the catch of the double is now very suspect."

7. Though many fine articles and portions of books have been devoted to her story, the standard work on Carrie Stevens is now Graydon Hilyard and Leslie Hilyard's beautifully produced and lavishly illustrated *Carrie Stevens, Maker of Rangeley Favorite Trout and Salmon Flies* (Mechanicsburg, PA: Stackpole Books, 2000). Despite a wealth of opinion and documentation to the contrary, George Leonard Herter, *Professional Fly Tying, Spinning and Tackle Making Manual and Manufacturer's Guide* (Waseca, MN: Herter's, revised nineteenth edition, 1971), 435, said that Carrie Stevens didn't originate the Gray Ghost. Herter believed that it was developed by a Montreal, Canada, tier named Pierre Dupont Wolfe and was called the Gray Ghost.

8. Henry Parkhurst Wells, "Fly-Fishing in the Rangeley Region," in Charles F. Orvis and A. Nelson Cheney, *Fishing with the Fly* (Boston: Houghton Mifflin, 1886), 97, said that "a guide is requisite to one unfamiliar to these waters. As far as surface indications are concerned, to a stranger one place looks about as promising as another; and the water area is so great, that only by the utmost good fortune could the best places be found."

9. Upon further examination, I have concluded that it looks most like a dark gray hyena.

10. Dave Whitlock, "Tactics for Tail-Water Trout," originally appeared in *Sports Afield*, April 1971, and was reprinted in Tom Paugh, ed., *The Sports Afield Treasury of Fly Fishing* (New York: Nick Lyons Books, 1989), 179–87. The quotation is from the book, 180.

11. Kenneth Owens, "Blue-Ribbon Tailwaters: The Unplanned Role of the U.S. Bureau of Reclamation in Western Fly Fishing," *The American Fly Fisher*, Spring 2007, 33 (2), 2–10. It was a matter of good fortune for me that just as I finished the two-part column in *American Angler* on which this chapter is based, I learned from Ken that he had a draft manuscript history of the tailwaters and was looking for a publisher, which he soon found in *The American Fly Fisher*. His attempts to sort out the process by which the tailwaters were "discovered" by managers and anglers were considerably more successful than mine, and I make use of his information here and there in the rest of this chapter.

12. There are "culture clashes" in the creation of these new fisheries as well. See for example Robert Behnke, "Tailwater Trout: Fish of Enormous Size," *Trout*, Spring 1996, 43–44. Owens, "Blue Ribbon Tailwaters," traced the role that the western tailwaters played in the rapid increase in interest in fly fishing in the American West after about 1975.

13. An informative policy analysis of the politics of modern dam management, with extensive historical context, is William R. Lowry, *Dam Politics: Restoring America's Rivers* (Washington, D.C.: Georgetown University Press, 2003). Owens, "Blue Ribbon Tailwaters," described in greater detail the chemical and biological processes by which a river is changed by a dam, including the ways that can work to the advantage of the enthusiastic fly fisher.

14. An excellent and popular book about the Columbia's modern human history is William Dietrich, *Northwest Passage: The Great Columbia River* (New York: Simon and Schuster, 1995), which I reviewed for *The New York Times Book Review*, June 4, 1995, 14. Another is Richard White, *The Organic Machine: The Remaking of the Columbia River* (New York: Hill and Wang, 1996).

15. For a concise summary of how dams affect a river see E. C. Pielou, *Fresh Water* (Chicago: University of Chicago Press, 1998), 205–13.

16. I recognize that there is not one "conservation movement" but many threads, interwoven yet distinct. The dams that I refer to here, Hetch Hetchy and Echo Park, were attacked primarily by advocates in the wilderness movement part of the conservation movement. I do not mean, at any point, to suggest a single-mindedness or unanimity among people who thought of themselves as conservationists, preservationists, sportsmen, nature lovers, and other parallel categories of people who in one way or another were concerned for the future of wildlife and its world in America.

17. For the Hetch Hetchy episode, see Robert Righter, *The Battle over Hetch-Hetchy: America's Most Controversial Dam and the Birth of Modern Environmentalism* (New York: Oxford University Press, 2005). John W. Simpson's *Dam!: Water, Power Politics, and Preservation in Hetch Hetchy and Yosemite National Park* (New York: Pantheon, 2005) advocates the removal of the dam and the restoration of the valley, which historical photographs suggest was only slightly less glorious a landscape than Yosemite Valley itself. For Echo Park, see Mark Harvey, *A Symbol of Wilderness: Echo Park and the American Conservation Movement* (Seattle: University of Washington Press, 2000).

18. Gasque, *Hunting and Fishing in the Great Smokies*, 100.

19. Montana Department of Fish, Wildlife & Parks, "Draft, Upper Bighorn River Fisheries Management Plan, December, 1986." Helena, Montana Department of Fish, Wildlife & Parks.

20. Chris Proctor, "New Perspectives on Fly Fishing," *Fly Fisherman*, December 1996, 28(1), 12.

21. Ibid.

22. Jeffrey W. Quinn and Thomas J. Kwak, "Fish Assemblage Changes in an Ozark River after Impoundment: A Long-Term Perspective," *Transactions of the American Fisheries Society*, 2003, 132:110–19. Owens, "Blue Ribbon Tailwaters," discussing this same phenomenon of change following the construction of a dam, pointed out that "On the Green River, for example, entomologists recorded 23 mayfly species before construction of the Flaming Gorge Dam. Now only four are documented," but they exist in nearly incredible abundance.

23. The era of dam removal campaigns, discussed in the following paragraphs, is the subject of Elizabeth Grossman, *Watershed: The Undamming of America* (Berkeley, CA: Counterpoint, 2002). Lowry, *Dam Politics*, also has discussions of both the Elwha and the Edmonds dams and the historical context of dam removals.

24. For a brief summary of the Elwha Dam story, see "Elwha River Washington" (no author), *Trout* magazine, Spring 2007, 19. For more information, see www.elwharivereducation.org.

As Ken Owens and others have reminded me in recent communications, we also need to temper our confidence in the river's ability to "heal" or "restore" itself. As Ken put it in a recent e-mail (July 18, 2006) to me, we need to ask ourselves what about "the dispersal of the accumulated silt burdens— often with lethal heavy metal concentrations—that you've earlier touched on, and the problems ameliorating other types of ecological damage done by the dams? What have we learned from the ongoing saga of reviving the Anaconda-poisoned Clark Fork? Do you suppose, in other words, that largely unaided natural processes will be sufficient to bring newly unchoked rivers back to a healthy condition? (Or will Haliburton, Wakan Tatanka forfend, need to step forward with a costly series of new engineering fixes?) Does the law of unintended consequences need to be considered?" Good questions.

25. Lowry, *Dam Politics*, 31. These are U.S. Army Corps of Engineers estimates.

CHAPTER SIX: OUTWORN PRIVILEGES

1. For a thorough history of Bozeman, see Phyllis Smith, *Bozeman and the Gallatin Valley: A History* (Helena, MT: Twodot, 1996). Though published more than a century ago, E. S. Topping's *The Chronicles of the Yellowstone* (Minneapolis: Ross & Haines, Inc., 1968 reprint with new introduction and notes by Robert Murray) is still a wonderful, colorful look at the earliest days of pioneering and settlement in the Yellowstone Valley. As for early Yellowstone sport, in a review of hundreds of early traveler's account of the area conducted by Yellowstone National Park Historian Lee Whittlesey and me during the past fifteen years, I have been amazed at how many early white travelers and residents fished for sport and food and how little study has been done of their activities in this respect.

2. "Good," Bozeman (Montana) *Avant Courier*, July 18, 1873, 3.

3. Paul Schullery, *Searching for Yellowstone: Ecology and Wonder in the Last Wilderness* (Boston: Houghton Mifflin Company, 1997), 68–84, and John Reiger, *American Sportsmen and the Origins of Conservation* (Corvallis, OR: Oregon State University Press, 2001), 126–45, described the early years of Yellowstone National Park wildlife management and the slaughter of park wildlife during that period.

4. It is surprising that for all its glamour and commerce, there is not yet a comprehensive history of trout fishing, much less of fly fishing, in Montana. In *Cowboy Trout* (Helena: Montana Historical Society Press, 2006), I provided references to some of the most important scholarly sources on certain aspects of Montana fly-fishing history, but these are hardly enough. The inadequacy of our appreciation of the sport's history in the West is the book's foremost lament.

5. Important historical sources on Yellowstone National Park include Aubrey Haines, *The Yellowstone Story*, two volumes (Boulder: Colorado Associated University Press, 1977); Richard Bartlett, *Yellowstone: A Wilderness Besieged* (Tucson:

University of Arizona Press, 1985); and Paul Schullery, *Searching for Yellowstone: Ecology and Wonder in the Last Wilderness* (Boston: Houghton Mifflin Company, 1997).

6. The most thorough reconsideration of the Washburn Party's attitudes and contributions to the creation of Yellowstone National Park is Paul Schullery and Lee Whittlesey, *Myth and History in the Creation of Yellowstone National Park* (Lincoln, NE: University of Nebraska Press, 2003). This discussion is based especially on Schullery and Whittlesey.

7. I'm not sure if he remained on the NPRR payroll after he was appointed superintendent of the park, but some historians, including the late Aubrey Haines and Lee Whittlesey, present park historian in Yellowstone National Park, are certain that during his superintendency the NPRR bosses influenced some of his management decisions to their own advantage and the disadvantage of park visitors. Langford rather notoriously refused to grant promising applicants for concessioner contracts with leases to operate in the park, apparently hoping to reserve those leases for railroad-controlled businesses.

8. Schullery, *Cowboy Trout*, 85.

9. This discussion is based primarily on Schullery, *Searching for Yellowstone*, and John D. Varley and Paul Schullery, *Yellowstone Fishes: Ecology, History, and Angling in the Park* (Mechanicsburg, PA: Stackpole Books, 1998).

10. Reiger, *American Sportsmen and the Origins of Conservation*, describes the central role played by sportsmen in the early years of wildlife conservation. The best history of the development of wildlife management in Yellowstone National Park is James Pritchard, *Preserving Yellowstone's Natural Conditions* (Lincoln: University of Nebraska, 1999).

11. Rudyard Kipling, *From Sea to Sea: Letters of Travel* (New York: Doubleday & McClure Company, 1899), 84.

12. Two good historical overviews of the development of fisheries management in Yellowstone National Park are Mary Ann Franke, "A Grand Experiment: 100 Years of Fisheries Management in Yellowstone," two parts, *Yellowstone Science*, Fall 1996, 2–7; Winter 1997, 8–13; and John Byorth, "Trout Shangri-La: Remaking the Fishing in Yellowstone National Park," *Montana: The Magazine of Western History* 52(2), 39–47. This issue of *Montana: The Magazine of Western History* is almost entirely devoted to fly-fishing history, and will lead you through its citations to other helpful sources.

13. Varley and Schullery, *Yellowstone Fishes*, 94–97.

14. Charles Adams, Director of the Roosevelt Wild Life Forest Experiment Station, in "The Relation of Wild Life to the Public in National and State Parks," *Roosevelt Wild Life Bulletin*, Volume 2, Number 4, February 1925, 382–83. For an overview of the development of fisheries management philosophy in the National Parks, see Paul Schullery, "A Reasonable Illusion," *Rod and Reel*, 1979, 5:44–54.

15. Most of us who follow this story would agree that the National Park Service, for all its gains in scientific credibility in selected parks, still must contend with

overpowering political and economic forces that can and often do defeat or deflect science-based decisions. We would also agree that there still isn't nearly enough scientific information available in almost all parks for managers to make the best possible decisions. For an influential review of the history of science in the national parks, see Richard Sellars, *Preserving Nature in the National Parks: A History* (New Haven: Yale University Press, 1999).

16. See Schullery, *Cowboy Trout*, 187–217, for a succinct overview of how we got into this fix.

17. This discussion is a review of material in previous publications by me, including "A Reasonable Illusion"; Varley and Schullery, *Yellowstone Fishes*; and *Searching for Yellowstone*.

18. As quoted in Schullery, "A Reasonable Illusion," 48.

19. Jane Kramer, "Blood Sport: How foxhunting became the most divisive issue in England," *The New Yorker*, January 24 & 31, 2005, 70–77.

CHAPTER SEVEN: IF FISH COULD SCREAM

1. Scott Adams, "Dilbert," as cited from the *Bozeman Daily Chronicle*, Bozeman, Montana, March 12, 2006. In another, undated "Dilbert" in my collection, the supervisor character says to a female employee, "I'm a nature lover. When I fish, I only do catch-and-release." She responds by saying, "In other words, you torture fish for fun."

2. John McPhee, *The Founding Fish* (New York: Farrar, Straus and Giroux, 2002), 309–34. McPhee's view, as persuasive as he obviously finds it, has roughly the same rhetorical force as most of the other positions on the topic, coming down more or less to "I'm right because I'm right." And that's true; he is without question right as far as his own values and needs are concerned. It's the angry intolerance for other possible stances that always makes these highly personal viewpoints so unconvincing.

3. On the matter of intention, and more generally for a rigorous consideration of the issues of cruelty in fishing, see the exchange of views in two papers, Dionys de Leeuw, "Contemplating the Interests of Fish: The Angler's Challenge," *Environmental Ethics* 18, 1996, 373–90; Len Olsen, "Contemplating the Intentions of Anglers: The Ethicist's Challenge," *Environmental Ethics* 25, Fall 2003, 267–77.

4. The study of the history and even the culture of blood sports has generated a rich if not especially large literature. All participants in serious dialogues over sport fishing owe it to the topic, their adversaries, and themselves to become at least nominally familiar with this literature. In the meantime, if you'd like a popularly written summary of some of the shortcomings of the typical knee-jerk attacks on sport fishing, I invite you to read my book *Real Alaska: Finding Our Way in the Wild Country* (Mechanicsburg, PA: Stackpole Books, 2001), especially 154–60, and 180–200.

5. Two extended popularly written discussions by fishing writers of cruelty and pain in fishing, both by British fishermen, are A. A. Luce, *Fishing and Thinking* (London: Hodder and Stoughton Lt., 1959), 170–91; and Bryn Hammond,

Halcyon Days: The Nature of Trout Fishing and Fishermen (Camden, ME: Ragged Mountain Press, 1992), 160–78. Both invoke numerous earlier authorities in favor of and against fishing as sport. Luce, the earlier writer, was ardently opposed to any practice similar to what we now call "catch-and-release" fishing. Hammond, writing more recently, was in the better position to quote modern animal-rights activists and attempt to respond to them. Both are stimulating, thoughtful, and sympathetic, and will be convincing to people who already believe the same things they do. A shorter but more eloquent statement on the same subject by an angler is Odell Shepard, *Thy Rod and Thy Creel* (New York: Nick Lyons Books, 1984 reprint of William Valentine Mitchell 1930 edition), 80–92. Far from being a subject that thoughtful anglers have hidden from, it seems to be one that some are drawn to.

6. James Rose, "The Neurobehavioral Nature of Fishes and the Question of Awareness and Pain," *Reviews in Fisheries Science* 2002, 10, 1–38. For a popular summary of this paper, see James Rose, "Do Fish Feel Pain?," *Fly Fisherman* 34(6), September 2003, 19–23.

7. Adrian Franklin, *Animals and Modern Cultures: A Sociology of Human-Animal Relations in Modernity* (London: Sage Publications, 1999), 12. It appears that for the millennia human societies have displayed concern over human cruelty to animals, most of their concern was directed at the humans. Such cruel behavior was of concern because of what it revealed about the character of the person mistreating the animals, and the humans were viewed as the most important element of the situation. Angling was condemned in part because of the opportunities it provided the unwary practitioner for misdeed and moral lapse.

8. See Franklin, *Animals in Modern Cultures*, 21–22, for some stimulating contrasts of interpretations of the cat-burning ritual.

9. Keith Thomas, *Man and the Natural World* (New York: Pantheon, 1983), 109–10.

10. Ibid., 189.

11. Peter Singer, *Animal Liberation: A New Ethics for Our Treatment of Animals* (New York: Avon Books, 1977 edition).

12. Paul Schullery, *Cowboy Trout: Western Fly Fishing As If It Matters* (Helena: Montana Historical Society Press, 2006), 193.

13. Dr. Martin Lluelyn, "Song Against Fishing," (originally published in 1646), reprinted from A. B. Shepperson, *An Angler's Anthology* (Charlottesville, VA: Madison Lane Press, University of Virginia, 1932), 10.

14. Ibid., 11.

15. There are still debates over the spawning question. One interesting example involves streams whose runs of salmon are entirely maintained by artificial means, through hatcheries. Some would argue that, because the spawning of the salmon will have no bearing on the future of the fish population, the spawning is irrelevant to ethical consideration. Others would argue that the spawning of the salmon is still a central element of the creature's individual existence, and deserves our respect for the intrinsic values of that quality alone. Most anglers don't seem to give it much thought. Biologically, there is only a thin line—

though it is a line that has held its place for a long time in sporting practice—between a salmon or other fish that is in the process of heading upstream toward its spawning grounds and one that has arrived. The former fish we feel perfectly comfortable trying to catch, and the latter we regard as inappropriate quarry. Much of angling's ethical framework seems to rest on such fine points; no wonder that it's so easy for the casual critic to take shots at it.

16. Leonard Mascall, *A Booke of Fishing with Hooke & Line* (London: John Wolfe, 1590), 15.
17. Ibid., 8.
18. Ibid., 15. The curious thing is that these dismemberings would seem to be counterproductive because they would dramatically reduce the ability of the live bait to struggle, and this attracts predators. In the New World, many generations of lure- and fly-makers have labored to devise ways to give their lures and flies life-like "action," so that a frog imitation seems to propel itself along with its legs, or a grasshopper imitation kicks and flutters on the surface of the water. Mary Orvis Marbury, *Favorite Flies and Their Histories* (New York: Houghton Mifflin Company, 1892), 118, said that "Any one who will invent a grasshopper with the natural 'kick' in it has a fortune in his hands."

On the other hand, there were practical rationales for mutilating these bait animals. Removal of legs would no doubt have left open wounds that bled, increasing the scent attraction of the lure, and perhaps the mutilated animal could still struggle, or even struggled more visibly. Besides, some of these baiting techniques were not really designed for motion; all anglers didn't want the bait moving around a lot.

19. Gervase Markham, *The Pleasures of Princes* (London: John Browne, 1614), 26. Both Mascall and Markham depended heavily on the *Treatise of Fishing with an Angle*, originally published in 1496.
20. James Chetham, *The Angler's Vade Mecum, or a Compendius, yet full, Discourse of Angling* (London: T. Basset and W. Brown, 1689), 315–16. I could have quoted Walton's similar advice on how to rig these baits; Chetham probably cribbed much of his bait material from Walton anyway. But in this case Chetham's narrative is the more explicit and gruesome, and I think the gruesomeness wanted full exposure here.
21. Gay is quoted from James Robb, *Notable Angling Literature* (London: Herbert Jenkins, Ltd., 1947; 1999 reprint, Ashburton, Devon: The Flyfisher's Classic Library, 1998), 103.
22. Ibid.
23. We can contrast this disapproval of draining the pond and, presumably, other non-angling ways of taking fish with other commentators who felt that netting and other methods that did not involve using hooks were inherently *less* cruel because they did not cause the pain that the hook was assumed to cause.
24. I discuss the history of the most common method of such natural-fly fishing, known as blow-line fishing, in *The Rise* (Mechanicsburg, PA: Stackpole Books,

2006), 161–64. For a charming recent treatment of this method of fishing, see Robert Boyle, *Dapping* (Mechanicsburg, PA: Stackpole Books, 2007).

25. Chetham's book, for all the thoroughness of its fly selection, has a lot more to say about arcane baits, handed down and accumulated from at least as many generations of bait fishers as the flies were from fly fishers.

26. Thomas, *Man and the Natural World*, 173.

27. Quoted in Henry S. Salt, *Animal's Rights Considered in Relation to Social Progress* (New York: MacMillan & Company, 1894), 113.

28. I have worked from a later Walton edition, Izaak Walton and Charles Cotton, *The Compleat Angler* (London: John Lane, 1897).

29. I take that to mean that the price was high in terms of the death of the sable, but I suppose it's possible that he was only commenting on how much it cost to buy the thing.

30. Joseph Sax's milestone study of the appropriate experience of wild nature in national parks, *Mountains Without Handrails: Reflections on the National Parks* (Ann Arbor: University of Michigan Press, 1980), 27–32, counts fly fishing, alone of all the blood sports, as a legitimate and even praiseworthy way to engage, personally and deeply, with the special wildness protected in national parks. Sax makes his case by quoting a variety of prominent historic and modern angling writers, including Izaak Walton, Arnold Gingrich, Alfred Miller ("Sparse Grey Hackle"), Norman MacLean, and Roderick Haig-Brown, and emphasizes the way in which fly fishing compels its practitioner to engage and explore the natural world for "the full involvement of the senses and the mind."

31. For an extended critique of the issues, see Adrian Franklin, *Animals and Modern Cultures: A Sociology of Human-Animal Relations in Modernity* (London: Sage Publications, 1999).

32. Thomas, *Man and the Natural World*, 177.

33. William Radcliffe, *Fishing from the Earliest Times* (London: Murray, 1921), 106–7.

34. Ibid. Hammond, *Halcyon Days*, 161, said that it was probably Walton's description of how to rig a small fish for bait—a description that, though more concise, was the same as Chetham's, quoted above—that led Byron to pen this verse. Hammond, 161, provides the full text of the note that Byron made about the verse and its recommendation

> It would have taught him humanity at least. This sentimental savage, whom it is a mode to quote (among novelists) to show their sympathy for innocent sports and old songs, teaches how to sew up frogs, and break their legs by way of experiment, in addition to the art of angling, the cruelest, the coldest, and the stupidest of pretended sports. They may talk about the beauties of Nature, but the angler merely thinks about his dish of fish; he has no leisure to take his eyes from off the streams, and a single bite is worth to him more than all the scenery around. Besides, some fish bite best on a

rainy day. The whale, the shark, and the tunny fishery have somewhat of noble and perilous in them; even net fishing, trawling, etc,
are more humane and useful. But angling! No angler can be a good
man.

For a defense of Walton more or less contemporary with Byron, see Edward
Jesse, *Scenes and Occupations of Country Life: With Recollections of Natural History*
(London: Murray, 1853).

35. Harriet Ritvo, *The Animal Estate: The English and Other Creatures in the Victorian
Age* (Cambridge: Harvard University Press, 1987), 126. See Ritvo especially for
excruciatingly detailed accounts of an incredible array of cruel practices that
were simply business as usual among most owners of domestic livestock
through much of the nineteenth century.

36. William Shipley, *A True Treatise on the Art of Fly-Fishing* (London: Simpkin, Mar-
shall, and Co., 1838), 8–9.

37. Sir Humphrey Davy, *Salmonia* (London: Murray, 1828), 11.

38. Ibid., 13.

39. Shipley, *A True Treatise on the Art of Fly-Fishing*, 10

40. Even if we try to think like a nineteenth-century person hearing Shipley's
story of the fish taking the hook baited with its own eye, we may still see the
contemporary weakness of his case. The shot bear may rush toward the hunter
who caused its pain. The beaten dog may turn on its abuser. People in the
nineteenth century, whose knowledge of animal nervous systems was primitive
at best and erroneous more often, could just as easily have argued that the fish
that attacked a hook or lure after having once escaped its pain was being
vengeful by continuing the fight. Such a theory, though flawed by today's standards because it presumed so many unwarranted things about fish consciousness, would be no better than, but probably no worse than, Shipley's
interpretation of such events. Shipley's arguments presumed that the fish must
recognize how a fish hook works, and would necessarily avoid a second
engagement with such a hook. That a fish might choose not to eat its own eye-
ball (a bait it had not encountered before) certainly would have been persuasive
proof of something important to Shipley's audience, in that no person would
have been willing to do such a thing. But the case too closely entangled the
natural impulses of a fish with the predilections of humans. The fish would
have no particular interest in or ability to recognize its own eye, nor would it
have a values system that prevented it from eating the flesh of its own species.
Shipley's story probably shocked his readers with the fish's "cannibalism," but
the charge of cannibalism was irrelevant in an animal species that had no evolutionary preparation for any other kind of behavior.

More or less contemporary with Shipley's statements was Harry Chol-
mondeley Pennell, *Can Fish Feel Pain?* (London: Warne, 1870), a small pam-
phlet by one of the most prominent angling writers of the late nineteenth
century. A more subtle and stimulating response to the charges of cruelty

appeared in a little-celebrated but nonetheless very thoughtful book from the early nineteenth century, Stephen Oliver, *Scenes and Recollections of Fly-Fishing* (London: Chapman and Hall, 1834), 45–58.

41. Reverend Oliver Raymond, *The Art of Fishing on the Principle of Avoiding Cruelty, with Approved Rules for Fishing Used During Sixty Years' Practice, Not Hitherto Published in Any Work on the Subject* (London: Longmans, Green, and Company, 1866).

42. Ibid., v.

43. Ibid., vii.

44. Ibid., 22.

45. Ibid., 32.

46. Ibid., viii.

47. Ibid., 67.

48. Ibid., 68.

49. Lynn White, "The Historical Roots of our Ecologic Crisis," *Science* 155, March 10, 1967.

50. Luce, *Fishing and Thinking*, 171–73, took a shot at reconciliation between angling and Christianity that isn't bad for its time and place. Hammond, *Halcyon Days*, 169–70, gave us a wonderful quote from fishing historian Conrad Voss Bark, who described attempting to argue about the morality of fishing with a man who was "a lay preacher and a vegetarian, a combination which together must be regarded as fairly formidable if one comes across them in an argument."

It would be well worth the time of a student of angling literature to conduct a review of issues of spirituality and religion as they surface here and there over the past few centuries. Though many of the better-known writers, from the *Treatyse* to Walton to Prime, invoke spiritual or religious sentiments as part of the fishing experience, there appear to be many lesser-known works, such as Raymond's, that need consulting. Among the earliest is Samuel Gardiner, *A Booke of Angling of Fishing. Wherein is showed, by conference with Scriptures, the agreement between the Fishermen, Fishes, and Fishing, of both Natures, Temporall and Spiritual* (London: Thomas Purfoot, 1606). In their masterful bibilographical study, *Bibliotheca Piscatoria, A Catalogue of Books on Angling, The Fisheries and Fish Culture* (London: W. Satchell, 1883), 41, 97, 138–39, 213, Thomas Westwood and Thomas Satchell inform us of a variety of texts that especially focus on this topic. There appears to be a disproportion of clergyman-angling writers in the literature, especially before 1900, and this is also a topic worth studying.

51. Luce, *Fishing and Thinking*, and Hammond, *Halcyon Days*, are about as good as we anglers have gotten at this in our fishing books. Luce was perhaps the more original, while Hammond may have covered the literature better. Between them, they will provide most of the major points that anglers have given in defense of fishing against the charge of cruelty. They also tell you which points seem to them to be most persuasive and which seem weak.

For a start at reading the more formally developed and scholarly literature, I suggest the following papers, from which readers can easily turn to the many papers and books they cite: the Rose article just mentioned, "Anthropomorphism and 'mental welfare' of fishes," *Diseases of Aquatic Organisms* 75, May 4, 2007, 139-154; two articles cited earlier: Dionys de Leeuw, "Contemplating the Interests of Fish: The Angler's Challenge," *Environmental Ethics* 18, 1996, 373-390, Len Olsen, "Contemplating the Intentions of Anglers: The Ethicists Challenge," *Environmental Ethics* 25, Fall 2003, 267-277; Robert Arlinghaus, Steven J. Cooke, Alexander Schwab, and Ian G. Crow, "Fish welfare: a challenge to the feelings-based approach, with implications for recreational fishing," *Fish and Fisheries* 8, 2007, 57-71; and Robert Arlinghaus, Steven J. Cooke, Jon Lyman, David Policansky, Alexander Schwab, Cory Suski, Stephen G. Sutton, and Eva B. Thorstad, "Understanding the Complexity of Catch-and-Release in Recreational Fishing: An Integrative Synthesis of Global Knowledge from Historical, Ethical, Social, and Biological Perspectives," *Reviews in Fisheries Science* 15, 2007, 75-167.

52. In Halford's time, fly fishers had not yet generally embraced barbless hooks specifically as a way to ease the capture and release of fish, but then we had not yet embraced catch-and-release fishing, either.

For an interesting modern attempt to identify the sources and nature of fly-fishing elitism, see Dennis Cutchins, "Elitism, Keeping Secrets, and Fly Fishing in Utah," *Western Folklore* 63: 1& 2 (Winter & Spring 2004), 189–202.

53. There is an entire book's-worth of thought, judgment, and opinion to be explored relating to that brief period of time between the moment that the fish is hooked and the moment the fish is landed. Angling literature suggests a vast range of feelings among anglers about the so-called "fight," from those who consider it the peak of the angling experience to those who wish it could somehow be avoided because they find it so unpleasant. I suspect that though so much of the criticism of angling has focused on the pain supposedly caused by the hook, at least as much of the real outrage is focused on how much anglers seem to enjoy the fish's struggle. Whether we personally perceive the fish's struggle as justifying some atavistic need in us—that is, literally as a natural and appropriate fight between us and the fish—or as a near-spiritual moment—that is, as a brief exhilarating connection between us and some otherwise untouchably remote natural wildness—or in some other way, the fight is what most troubles a lot of our critics. One often-noticed irony here is that while many fly fishers regard the skillful capture of a large fish on necessarily light terminal tackle as a great achievement, and though when such a fish is feeding on extremely small flies that may be the only way to take it, such tackle may lead to the extreme exhaustion or death of the fish. The "best" or "prettiest" fishing, by our current definitions, may be the hardest on the fish.

54. McPhee, *The Founding Fish*, 321.

55. Ken Cameron, e-mail to the author, March 19, 2006.

56. The most rhetorically hairy-chested, self-described atavists defend their hunting and fishing as an authentic animal need; they say they hunt because they are members of a hunting species, which is to say that they hunt because they must. These days, most observers aren't impressed with this argument, but even if the atavism is overstated there is still much to be gained—spiritually, emotionally, intellectually—by such humbling, exhilarating, and elemental participation in another creature's most basic struggle for existence. At least, many anglers would say there is.

57. This is probably the view that has been most eloquently expressed by angling's philosopher-writers, who describe the joys of fishing indirectly, in terms of all the things that have to do with it but may not have to do with actually hooking the fish. It's a big picture out there on the river, and the fish are often few and far between. Many other things enrich us and keep us going while we wait.

58. Shepard, *Thy Rod and Thy Creel*, 116–17.

59. Quoted in Salt, *Animals' Rights*, 14–15.

60. Though I do not recall if he ever put it into print, I believe that I first heard this statement made by the West Yellowstone fly-fishing writer Charles Brooks.

INDEX